God's Methods With Man

God's Methods With Man

In Time: Past, Present and Future . .

By the Rev.
G. CAMPBELL MORGAN
Author of "Discipleship," etc.

Wipf & Stock
PUBLISHERS
Eugene, Oregon

Wipf and Stock Publishers
199 W 8th Ave, Suite 3
Eugene, OR 97401

God's Methods with Man
In Time: Past, Present, and Future
By Morgan, G. Campbell
ISBN 13: 978-1-59244-380-2
ISBN 10: 1-59244-380-X
Publication date 10/2/2003
Previously published by Fleming H. Revell Company, 1898

Author's Note

THESE addresses were delivered in substance at Northfield, and reported stenographically. They were then revised and expanded, and were afterward delivered in my own church. A flood of letters, books, and pamphlets poured in upon me: some from enquirers; some from those who have differed from positions taken up; and very many from those who have been helped.

These letters have all been acknowledged, except in cases where that was rendered impossible by anonymity. However, I was and am determined not to be tempted into controversy of any kind, either by letter or in print, seeing that I am far from claiming that hearers or readers are bound to accept my convictions as absolute truth. I simply desire to enunciate what I believe to be the teaching of the New Testament.[1] The final court of appeal is not any man's interpretation, but God's Book; and I may have something yet to learn upon certain points.

If those whom I address search the Scriptures

[1] The quotations are from the Revised Version.

for proof of my statements, and do not come to the same conclusions as myself, we may yet rejoice together in that we shall thereby know the Word of God more perfectly, and moreover that "what we know not now, we shall know hereafter."

G. CAMPBELL MORGAN.

New Court Chapel,
    Tollington Park, N.

CONTENTS

I
INTRODUCTORY 9

II
FROM CREATION TO CHRIST 15

III
THE DISPENSATION OF THE SPIRIT 29

IV
THE COMING OF CHRIST 47

V
DANIEL'S MISSING WEEK 67

VI
THE EVENTS OF THE MISSING WEEK 81

VII
THE DAWN OF A GOLDEN AGE 97

VIII
THE GOLDEN AGE 113

IX
AFTER THE THOUSAND YEARS 129

X
THE PURIFYING HOPE 145

APPENDIX 161

Ere God had built the mountains,
　Or raised the fruitful hills;
Before He filled the fountains
　That feed the running rills—
In Me, from everlasting,
　The wonderful I AM,
Found pleasures, never wasting;
　And Wisdom is My name.

When, like a tent to dwell in,
　He spreads the skies abroad,
And swathed about the swelling
　Of ocean's mighty flood—
He wrought by weight and measure;
　And I was with Him then:
Myself the Father's pleasure,
　And Mine, the sons of men.

Thus Wisdom's words discover
　Thy glory and Thy grace,
Thou everlasting Lover
　Of our unworthy race.
Thy gracious eye surveyed us,
　Ere stars were seen above;
In wisdom Thou hast made us,
　And died for us in love.

And couldst Thou be delighted
　With creatures such as we—
Who, when we saw Thee, slighted
　And nailed Thee to a tree?
Unfathomable wonder,
　And mystery divine!
The voice that speaks in thunder
　Says—"Sinner, I am thine!"

　　　　　　　　　　COWPER.

God's Methods with Man

I

INTRODUCTORY

FOR a correct estimate of the present times, and a true conception of future events, we must have a clear understanding of the things that are past. We are in danger of living too much in the present, and of looking upon the Divine activities as if they were haphazard or accidental, as our own always are, save as we are under the control of the Spirit of God. We seem to have contracted the idea that in the history of the race God has been making experiments with men; and that when one plan has failed, He has adopted another. Such false conceptions arise from the fact that, mentally and spiritually, we live too much in the circle of our own times, and are forgetful of all that has gone before. The corrective is found in studying history from the Divine standpoint. Nothing yields a more chaotic, uncertain, and unsatisfactory result than a view merely from the human side; while, on the contrary, order, beauty, and progress, are seen only as we take the Divine outlook.

The Chart which accompanies these Lectures is intended as an aid to the mind through the avenue of the eye. It is a comparatively simple delineation of the events with which we have to deal, and is intended to represent the whole stream of time. The portion of a circle colored blue represents the past eternity. The beginning of time is marked by a small green circle, signifying a state of earthly perfection, the garden of Eden as it came from the hand of God. Human history runs on in epochs— from the Fall of man to the Flood; from the Flood to the call of Abraham; from the call of Abraham to Moses; and the reign of Law to the coming of Christ. From the point where human sin begins, the red line marks the presence of sacrifice, the blood of "the Lamb slain from the foundation of the world." At the end of the period of Law, the Cross is uplifted; and a line ascending indicates the return of Jesus to the heavens. So far as humanity is concerned, that line is black, announcing the culmination of sin; and, in contrast, we have the gold which tells of heavenly glory accomplished by that Cross of Jesus Christ. A circle, showing the sphere of the Holy Spirit's dispensation, is colored red, because the whole earth to-day, as viewed from the Divine standpoint, is under the blood of Christ's Cross. God is dealing with man, entirely and everywhere, under the shelter and shadow of that Cross. A thin, green line from Eden to Calvary marks the fact that throughout human history God has never left the earth without witnesses who have been loyal to Him. That line becomes, in the period of the Spirit's work, a golden one; for the testimony is now of a heavenly, as distinct from the former earthly, character. A line half gold, half purple, indicates the priestly work of Jesus Christ in the heavens during this period. The device of a tongue of fire represents the Spirit as connecting the exalted Christ and the earth on which we live. This dispensation ends with the coming of Christ, and the ascent of the Church to meet Him, marked by a line, the black of which signifies the mystery of the rapture to the unregenerate, and the blue and gold, the glory the Church now enters upon with Christ. Then sets in a short period of tribulation upon the earth, indicated by a black section; at the end of which Christ and His Church come to the mid-heavens; He Himself descends to the earth; and we have the Millennium, a green circle with the star of gold, showing that while an earthly glory is set up, the Kingdom of Heaven will be realized under the direct rule of Christ and His people. The red line of blood is taken up and continued on our Chart immediately upon the end of this dispensation. At the end of the Millennium there will be a short period of further trouble upon the earth, again marked by a black section. A golden section indicates the fullness of the times, the glorious reign of Christ, and then the great eternities set in, when God shall be all in all.

It is well to approach this subject reverently, humbly, and apart from controversy. The Bible we shall regard throughout as the authoritative revelation of God concerning His dealings with men. We shall turn neither to the right hand nor to the left to defend the statements of the Word of God.

At the outset, however, there are certain principles to which assent must be given, in order to a true understanding of the whole scheme of these studies.

I. First, the one abiding, eternal, unchangeable fact — *God is*. It is necessary thus to get down to the bed-rock for a sound structure.

II. Then we must recognize the truth of Divine Sovereignty. The God from Whose thought all good things come, has never handed over anything to other government than His own. It may be that, for awhile, the prince of the power of the air has seemed to rule; but let it never be forgotten that God is upon His throne, high and lifted up, still holding in His hands the reins of government. Not only in His own heavens, not only on this earth, but in the deepest abyss itself, God is absolutely Sovereign.

III. The next point is that this rule cannot be set aside; it will continue forever, notwithstanding all opposition.

IV. Lastly, because God is, and because He still holds the reins of government, there must come the final triumph of His Kingdom and of His will.

II

From Creation to Christ

I looked : aside the dust-cloud rolled—
  The Waster seemed the Builder too;
Upspringing from the ruined Old
      I saw the New.

'T was but the ruin of the bad,—
  The wasting of the wrong and ill;
Whate'er of good the old time had
      Was living still.

    .   .   .   .   .   .

The outworn rite, the old abuse,
  The pious fraud transparent grown,
The good held captive in the use
      Of wrong alone—

These wait their doom, from that great law
  Which makes a past time serve to-day;
And fresher life the world shall draw
      From their decay.

    .   .   .   .   .   .

But life shall on and upward go;
  Th' eternal step of Progress beats
To that great anthem, calm and slow,
      Which God repeats.

    .   .   .   .   .   .

God works in all things: all obey
  His first propulsion from the night:
Wake thou and watch!—the world is grey
      With morning light!

                      J. G. WHITTIER.
                          "*The Reformer.*"

II

FROM CREATION TO CHRIST

In thought we enter the dread silence of eternity past; and as the voices of earth are hushed, we have in that silence one consciousness—God is love. Every movement of creation began there.

"In the beginning God *created* the heaven and the earth."

The phrase "the beginning" carries us behind all dates. The first certainty is that God created—*when*, no man can tell: *how far back*, is beyond all computation. Behind the beginning of material things—God. Those who would put science and revelation in opposition say to us, "You tell us that the world is six thousand years old; but here is a piece of rock which must be thousands of years older." We reply that we do not count our six thousand years from the creation of matter, but from that of man. Your rock may be as old as you please. Our claim is that, beyond your longest stretch of years, is God—creating. Yet another change—"The earth was waste and void; darkness was upon the face of the waters."

It may be well to tabulate the statements of Genesis i. 1, 2:

1. "In the beginning God."

The only satisfactory statement possible concerning the countless ages of the past. The light of the New Testament enables us to make a further assertion concerning that past eternity, viz, " God is love."

2. " God created the heaven and the earth."

That declares the origin of all of which we know anything beside God Himself. No date is fixed, nor can be.

3. "The earth was waste and void, and darkness was upon the face of the deep."

Between this and the former, some unchronicled event has transpired; for " waste and void " are words which cannot describe the first conditions of any creation of God.

4. "The Spirit of God moved upon the face of the waters."

The chaotic earth was not God-forsaken, but watched by the unwearying vigilance of the Eternal Spirit. How long this lasted none can tell.

We come now to a point with which we are more immediately concerned, " And God *said*." Here we have for the first time Divine thought expressed in speech. The Word of God, the *Logos*. In John's Gospel is an important statement bearing on this fact—John i. 1:

"In the beginning was the Word, and the Word was with God, and the Word was God."

By the *Logos* God brings order out of disorder, and beauty out of the darkness. The Word of God sounded over the chaotic earth; and, in response to that Word, there arose order, beauty, everything that we see to-day, only in its perfection. Read in this connection, Prov. viii., where the Word of God is spoken of as Wisdom. Observe the declarations of that wonderful passage, that in all God's creative acts, "I (Wisdom) was daily His delight." Thus we have creation by God, through Christ, the Wisdom or the Word of God; the earth thoroughly furnished, and man placed thereon. So time begins.

Accepting absolutely the Bible story, which fits in with reason, experience, and hope, we find man created in the image of God and placed amid perfect environment. He lives in the Divine favor, holding unbroken communion with God, and dwelling in the realm of loyalty to Him. Some say that man was a non-moral being until he fell; but we contend that the moment he stood in the garden of Eden, with its testing point for character in the forbidden tree, and the Divine denial of its fruit upon his soul, he knew that the realms of right and of wrong were bounded by obedience and disobedience. He was a moral being the moment he took up his position there. God did not tempt, but tested, man—an absolute necessity in the nature of the case, for man is a being with a will. Man's will is paralyzed, robbed of its glory and magnificence, save as he has opportunity to use it.

Tennyson says

> "Our wills are ours, we know not how;
> Our wills are ours to make them Thine."

But man chose to make his will his own, in contradiction to the Divine will; becoming, by that action, immoral. He fell, was driven forth; and, from that moment, the reign of conscience set in. Man took his place outside the garden of Eden, to face the future with its conflict and need. His position was that of a sinner; and the Divine dealing was no longer with one innocent, but with a law-breaker. Straightway the blood line was over the earth, pointing to the Lamb slain from the foundation of the world, and to be slain in the fullness of time. God brought to the man and woman in the garden coats of skins; and there could have been no such clothing save as there had first been the sacrifice of life and the shedding of blood. The sacrifices, which ever pointed on to Christ's Cross, began here with man's sin. Man went out from the garden, with his hope set on the future, comforted by the announcement that the seed of the woman should bruise the serpent's head. God sent into life new ministries of sorrow and toil, that man might, by the consciousness of loss, be drawn back to the Divine heart.

The story of the earth from Eden to the Flood, covering about 1665 years, is known to us all. During that period two races of men were developed. First, we have the line from Adam through Cain, tending to corruption and degradation. There is also the line through Seth, which culminates in Enoch, at the seventh generation, who "walked with God, and was not, for God took him."

From Enoch the line of demarcation became less and less distinct until in the days of Noah humanity had reached an awful depth of degradation. Gen. vi. 11, 5:

"And the earth was corrupt before God, and the earth was filled with violence." "And the Lord saw that the wickedness of man was great in the earth, and that every imagination of the thoughts of his heart was only evil continually."

God now destroyed the whole race by the Flood, with the exception of an elect company, by whom the continuity of the race was preserved, and on whom a new era had dawned.

Hitherto man's conscience had been under blood. Blood and sacrifice still held their place, but God imposed upon man the duty of mutual self-government. Let us turn to one passage only, in Gen. ix. 5, 6:

> "Surely your blood, the blood of your lives, will I require; at the hand of every beast will I require it: and at the hand of man, even at the hand of every man's brother, will I require the life of man. Whoso sheddeth man's blood, by man shall his blood be shed: for in the image of God made He man."

That is a new arrangement. Men are now to be governed mutually. Every man is to exercise care for his brother: and if man slay his brother-man, other men are to see that he pays the penalty with his life. Thus God safeguards the life of each by making all responsible for the lives of individuals. It is a new commencement, with corruption and evil put away by the Flood.

Soon after the Deluge, the tower of Babel rose. Some assert that its object was security against the effects of any future flood. Gen. xi. 4 shows, however, the thought in the minds of the builders.

> "Go to, let us build us a city, and a tower, whose top may reach unto heaven, and let us make us a name; *lest we be scattered abroad upon the face of the whole earth.*"

It was not that they hoped to escape another

From Creation to Christ

judgment which might be coming upon them; but they desired solidarity. To-day we hear a great deal about the "solidarity of humanity"; and the endeavor to secure it by putting God out of His own world is a very old piece of history. Apart from Him, the only really cohesive force for humanity is absent, and confusion must be the result. These men were scattered throughout the whole earth, and their tongues were confounded. Some of our friends are seeing very serious difficulties to-day as regards that confusion of tongues. Personally, I see no more objection to this record than to the account of the Pentecostal gift of tongues; and if men are prepared to question one, why not the other?

Here there came into human history the element of nationality. We talk proudly to-day about our patriotism. Patriotism is after all one of the greatest curses the world has ever seen, and is but another name for selfishness. What is the Divine ideal? "He hath made of *one blood all the nations* of the earth." All nationality and patriotic pride have sprung from Babel, and the attempt to do without God. Supposing all nationality were swept from the world to-day, what would follow? Disarmament, and peace. Then there would be real unity; and until that is realized, "brotherhood" outside the Christian Church is an anomaly and foolishness. God scattered these Babel builders in their attempt to secure solidarity without Him.

From Babel to Abraham there was a development of national pride, self-interest, and consequent animosities. In the call of Abraham, we find God taking one man upon the principle of faith. Faith is the confidence of man in God, which results in his submission and obedience. The world had lost this principle, and, as we have seen, the latest unfolding of unbelief was the attempt to secure unity apart from the Divine. As a result the solidarity of the race was lost, and a company of nations, with prejudices, and pride, began to conflict with each other. God's purpose in calling Abraham was that of creating a new nation, held together by this unifying principle of faith, that through them the nations of the earth might learn the blessedness and peace of the Divine Kingship.

That is the true story of the calling of Abraham and the creation of Israel as a nation. I solemnly protest against the common mistake concerning the calling of Israel to God's service, that God abandoned the world, and took but a few people for Himself. God called Abraham and said, "I will bless thee and make thee a blessing; and in thee shall all the nations of the earth be blessed." As at the first God's Spirit brooded over chaos before order was evolved therefrom, so His unwearied love never ceases toward man. Israel was created to influence other nations for God, itself being within His kingdom. Israel, however, rebelled against God's rule; and ended in Egypt and in slavery. Through unbelief and sin, the whole nation went down into bondage.

After four hundred years, God wrought deliverance for them; and then the period of Law set in, and the nation was brought under the direct Kingship of God. Thus was instituted the most marvellous government the world has ever seen. Very wonderful was that period in the wilderness, when a great and mighty people were trained as God's children, and were prepared for all that lay before them. Their law was given them by God, and they lived within its sphere.

They came into the promised land, and then degeneracy set in. They grew tired of theocracy, and demanded a monarchy. We have a King, said they, but He is in the heavens; these nations have kings who are with them in courts, robes, and palaces. Give us such an one! They had their desire, and passed through earthly kingship into the realm of corruption, and ultimately into renewed captivity. At last God's kingly rule passed from them altogether; and the times of the Gentiles set in, with Media, Persia, Greece, and Rome, in the ascendant.

Still the line of witnesses for God ran on, in a few souls true to Him, such as Anna, Simeon, the shepherds, and others who looked for the day of the Messiah.

Now came the last message, that of John, followed by the King Himself with the same words, "The kingdom of heaven is at hand." He declared its laws, and gave evidences of its benefactions, as He healed men, drove out devils, and applied heaven's solace to earth's sorrows and travail for His brief ministry of three and a half years. How did it end? "He came unto His own, and they that were His own received Him not," but gave Him the death of the Cross.

The evident lessons of our study are two— first, *human failure;* second, *Divine progress.* Look where you will in human history, you find failure. The Fall and the Flood, Corruption and the Cross. Every time humanity is put upon a new footing it fails. Has God failed? Not once; everything has been preparatory and progressive. Let us retrace our steps. The Cross and all that it means was prepared for throughout Judaic history. This one nation of Israel learned, through battle and smoke, murmuring and forgiveness, captivity and deliverance, the great truth that there is but one God. Monotheism is the lesson which humanity has learned through Israelitish history. From the time when Israel came back out of Babylon, she never again set up idols. When that truth was enshrined for the world in the chosen nation, then the one God became flesh. God was preparing through the wonderful history of their times for the Incarnation. What of the failure that preceded the Flood? Sin worked itself out to the utmost head of corruption. God allowed it to have its own free working, and then He swept it away, and started man upon the next stage of history, having behind him that terrific example of what sin is when it is left to its own course. I am bold to say that human corruption, so far as its actual effects upon men's lives are concerned, has never reached the awful depths of degradation which prevailed before the flood, when the sons of men were holding intercourse with evil spirits.

Thus we have sin manifested and the one God seen; while the Incarnate Word takes that sin upon Himself, that the world may ever know, from that point onward, the meaning of sin as well as the meaning of God and His Divine government.

III

The Dispensation of the Spirit

When God of old came down from heaven,
　　In power and wrath He came;
Before His feet the clouds were riven,
　　Half darkness and half flame.

　　.　　.　　.　　.　　.　　.

But when He came the second time,
　　He came in power and love;
Softer than gale at morning prime
　　Hover'd His Holy Dove.

The fires that rushed on Sinai down
　　In sudden torrents dread,
Now gently light, a glorious crown,
　　On every sainted head.

Like arrows went those lightnings forth,
　　Winged with the sinner's doom;
But these, like tongues o'er all the earth,
　　Proclaiming life to come.

And as on Israel's awe-struck ear
　　The voice, exceeding loud,
The trump, that angels wake to hear,
　　Thrilled from the deep, dark cloud;

So, when the Spirit of our God
　　Came down His flock to find,
A voice from heaven was heard abroad,
　　A rushing, mighty wind.

　　.　　.　　.　　.　　.　　.

It fills the Church of God; it fills
　　The sinful world around;
Only in stubborn hearts and wills
　　No place for it is found.
　　　　　　　　　KEBLE.
　　　　　　　　　　"*Christian Year.*"

III

THE DISPENSATION OF THE SPIRIT

WE now come to deal with the central circle in our Chart, marking the present dispensation. The thin line continued across it, is golden instead of green, showing that God's chosen people are now of heavenly, rather than earthly, character. Above is a line which marks the present High Priestly work of Jesus Christ in the heavens, this line having its purple or priestly side toward the earth. The device of a divided tongue of fire shows that the whole dispensation is that of the Spirit.

Let me remind you of the events immediately following the crucifixion of Jesus Christ. There was the resurrection from among the dead; and then the forty days which He spent among His disciples, every day of which undoubtedly had some very definite meaning. It is of the greatest interest to trace His appearances during that period to various persons, upon different occasions, in different places and ways. The ten days of waiting, between His ascension and the ushering in of the Spirit's dispensation, were for the disciples days of weakness and of foolishness. These men whom

Christ had called to Himself had no wisdom to know what to do, even if they had possessed the power to accomplish anything. God, in infinite wisdom, left them for ten days, enjoining them to wait for "the promise of the Father," and until they were endued with "power from on high." We are all familiar with the story of Pentecost and its effects upon these men in the upper room: the rushing mighty wind, filling the whole house where they were assembled, and the appearance of parting tongues of fire sitting upon each of them. The wondrous power, that came upon Christ's followers, the new Spirit that possessed them, and the marvellous deeds of early apostolic days are well known to every one of us. It is our aim to get a general view of the whole dispensation thus inaugurated.

By His coming at the day of Pentecost upon that company of men and women in the upper room, the Holy Ghost *formed* the Church of Jesus Christ. There had been no Church prior to that coming of the Spirit. Individual Jewish disciples had gathered around the Lord during the days of His ministry, and He prepared them for the ushering in of this wondrous dispensation. As they gathered together day by day in the upper room, they were a collection of separate individual souls; but "when the day of Pentecost was fully come," and the

Spirit fell upon them, He united them into one whole body, the Church of Jesus Christ. The Spirit came to create the Church, to be the bond of its life; and, from that time to this, men have only entered the Church of Jesus Christ through the new creation of the Spirit. Avoiding anything like controversy, we still find it necessary to say in passing, that no person was ever admitted to the Church of Jesus Christ by water baptism, or by votes of members. There can be no admission into spiritual union by that which is purely material. We admit persons into Church fellowship, not in order that they may become members of the Church of Christ, but because they are already such. For the sake of a very important distinction, I repeat that by the coming of the Spirit the Church was *formed;* and that same Spirit has, from that day to this, admitted into the Church of Jesus Christ such souls as, convinced by Himself, have believed upon Christ and have been therefore born again of the Spirit. So began the dispensation in which we live.

What is the difference between the Spirit's relation to this present dispensation and to former ones? This question is very important; because we are in danger of imagining that God has, in some way, been working in sections of Himself while dealing with men. This is not so: the Spirit had direct dealings with every dispensation that has passed away. Psalm xxxiii. 6:

"By the word of the Lord were the heavens made;
And all the host of them by the breath of His mouth."

There can be very little doubt that, in order to carry the true sense of the word there to English readers, *breath* should have a capital *B*, as referring to the Holy Spirit; and, in that declaration of the Psalmist, we have the union of God the Father, with the Word of God, and the Spirit of God in creation. Gen. vi. 3:

"And the Lord said, My Spirit shall not strive with man forever, for that he also is flesh."

I do not refer you to that verse to deal with it in its setting, to which I make only passing reference. It is continually being quoted as applicable to this dispensation and to individual life therein. Sermons have been preached from this passage, to prove that God now withdraws His Spirit from living men. Such use is contrary to Scripture, and a denial of the great lines of order upon which God proceeds and from which He never deviates in His dealings with men. In its setting, it plainly refers, some one hundred and twenty years before the event, to the time when judgment should set in by the Flood. But I quote it to show that in the old dispensation God dealt with man by His Spirit for special reasons and on particular occasions. Num. xi. 25:

> "And the Lord came down in the cloud, and spake unto him, and took of the Spirit that was upon him, and put it upon the seventy elders; and it came to pass that when the Spirit rested upon them, they prophesied."

The Authorized Version adds, "and did not cease"; but the Revised Version makes an important alteration, "they did so no more." The elders only prophesied when the Spirit was upon them. We read further that when Eldad and Medad, who were not ordained, began prophesying (verses 27-29):

> "There ran a young man, and told Moses, and said, Eldad and Medad do prophesy in the camp. And Joshua the son of Nun, the minister of Moses, one of his chosen men, answered and said, My lord Moses, forbid them. And Moses said unto him, Art thou jealous for my sake? Would God that all the Lord's people were prophets."

Why did these men prophesy? Because the Spirit of God had come upon them. The Spirit on the elders made them prophets; but when He was taken from them, they ceased to prophesy. Forgive the use of a word to which I particularly object, but I employ it in its common acceptation: the Spirit upon the *laity* made them prophets. (It is high time that we drop the unholy distinction between clergy or ministers and "the laity"). The Spirit came, of old, that men, in or out of orders as God chose, should become His messengers to the age in which they lived.

Another interesting reference to the work of the Spirit in the old dispensation occurs in Exodus xxxi. 1-5:

> "And the Lord spake unto Moses, saying, See, I have called by name Bezalel, the son of Uri, the son of Hur, of the tribe of Judah: and I have filled him with the Spirit of God." *What for?* "In wisdom, and in understanding, and in knowledge, and in all manner of workmanship, to devise cunning works, to work in gold, and in silver, and in brass, and in cutting of stones for setting, and in carving of wood, to work in all manner of workmanship."

The anointing of the Spirit to be a brassworker, carpenter, stonecutter, and everything else! Would to God we believed it, in this day, more than we do! In the old dispensation, men who had special work to do were fitted for it, even to the details of material things, by the coming upon them of the Spirit of God. Such illustrations might be multiplied; and they form a most interesting study.

Under the old dispensation the Spirit was given to certain men for specific work or the delivery of special messages; and when the work was done, He was withdrawn. He was then, if I may use the phrase, a visitor to men, coming by the will of God, accomplishing the Divine purpose. But godly men of those days

The Dispensation of the Spirit 37

looked for something further, even in connection with the Spirit of God. Here is a prophecy containing a promise made to them:

> Joel ii. 28-30: "And it shall come to pass afterward, that I will pour out My Spirit upon all flesh; and your sons and your daughters shall prophesy, your old men shall dream dreams, your young men shall see visions: and also upon the servants and upon the handmaids in those days will I pour out My Spirit."

That was a promise made to the old dispensation, but not fulfilled in it; and it is a supreme instance, but not the only one, of such a promise. Jer. xxxi., and the wondrous chapters toward the close of Ezekiel's prophecy, show how men of old waited, not only for the coming Messiah, but for the giving of the Holy Ghost, as never before.

From Creation through the reign of conscience, on to the period of law, the Spirit worked among men upon occasion, convincing of sin, revealing the will of God, fitting for specific service to be rendered to God; but that was all. Pentecost, however, was a fulfillment of the prophecy in Joel. Peter, speaking to the assembled crowd concerning the sights which they had seen and the sounds which they had heard, said, in answer to a criticism from some in that crowd (Acts ii. 14-16):

> "Ye men of Judæa, and all ye that dwell at Jerusalem, be this known unto you, and give ear unto my

words. For these are not drunken, as ye suppose; seeing it is but the third hour of the day; but this is that which hath been spoken by the prophet Joel."

At Pentecost the Holy Spirit came in His fullness as He had never come before, to be for this dispensation not a visitor but a resident in the Church. That event was equal in importance to the Incarnation itself, was closely allied to it, and was its direct consequence. Bring together those remarkable statements: "The Word was made flesh"; "I will pour out my Spirit upon all flesh." Now that Divinity has come to humanity, and humanity in the person of the incarnate *Logos* is linked to Divinity— the Spirit of God can be poured out upon all flesh. The two events are so closely joined in essence that neither can be correctly understood apart from the other. By the coming of that Spirit on the day of Pentecost as the result of the finished work of the Son of God, we enter upon the Spirit's dispensation—that in which we live to-day.

The Holy Spirit is to-day the Revealer and the Administrator of the absent King Whom the world still rejects. Never let it be forgotten that we are living in a world which has cast out the King. We are the direct descendants of the people who joined in saying, "We will not have this Man to reign over us." The fact that the earth has cast Him out abides unto

The Dispensation of the Spirit 39

this time; but God, in grace, has turned the wrath of man into that which praises Him, taking hold of human failure and transforming it into Divine victory. The heavens have received the King for a time; but while He is hidden from the eyes of men for awhile, the Living One is being made real to all peoples of the earth in this generation. How? By the living Spirit, the Holy Spirit of God, the Administrator of the King in His absence. He makes Christ, and not Himself, the consciousness of the believer. His one work is to uplift, unveil, reveal Jesus to the hearts of His people; to realize within the character of those who are born again all Jesus is, by bringing them under the blessed rule of the King Himself.

Sometimes friends ask me to recommend them a book upon the Holy Spirit. My reply is, "Read John's Gospel, chapters xiv. to xvi.; for there you have weighty statements concerning the Holy Ghost from the lips of the Master Himself." Take xiv. 16:

> "I will make request of the Father, and He shall give you another Comforter."

In Scripture there are untranslatable words, having in them infinite depths of meaning, which can never be put into any number of words; and this term, "the Comforter," is one of them. You may make it "Intercessor" or "Advocate," if you will; but it means both, and infinitely more than the two together. It is the word which reveals the work of the Spirit in the life of the believer. Verses 16, 17:

> "And I will pray the Father, and He shall give you another Comforter, that He may be with you forever, even the Spirit of truth: Whom the world cannot receive; for it beholdeth Him not, neither knoweth Him: ye know Him; for He abideth with you, and shall be in you."
>
> Verse 26.—"But the Comforter, even the Holy Spirit, Whom the Father will send in My name, He shall teach you all things, and bring to your remembrance all that I said unto you."

So that the one work of the Spirit of God is to teach things concerning Christ, and to bring to remembrance and understanding the words which fell from His lips. This proves that there is a twofold aspect of the Spirit's work— a truth which I can now only outline. First, there is His work in the world and with the people of the world; and then there is His work in the Church and with the people of the Church. Read the word of the apostle in 1. Tim. iv. 10:

> "For to this end we labor and strive, because we have our hope set on the living God, Who is the Saviour of all men, specially of them that believe."

We see, then, that the work of *Jesus Christ* has a twofold aspect—He is the Saviour of all

The Dispensation of the Spirit 41

men, He is the Saviour specially of those who believe. If therefore the Spirit of God comes to take up Christ's work, to apply it and make Him real, the same double office will characterize the Spirit's operations. Because we have lost sight of this truth, some have fallen away from the hope of the Church—the return of our Lord Himself.

First, there is the work of the Spirit in the Church; then His work upon all flesh. Referring again to Acts ii., the Spirit fell—upon whom? Upon the waiting disciples, baptizing them in His fullness, filling them as He came, equipping them for life and for service by His coming, creating by that inflow the Church. But presently the little company broke up and went from the upper room, and as Peter preached to the crowd, the people were moved and swayed. How? By Peter's preaching? Assuredly not. If Peter had preached the day before, he might have uttered the same words, but they would not have produced that effect. How, then, was the crowd swayed? The Spirit of God was dealing with it; for Peter's preaching was in power and in demonstration of the Spirit. What is demonstration? Making plain. Peter uttered what he had to declare—his witness concerning the Master—and the Spirit made it plain to those who heard. It is such demonstration of the Spirit which still marks the true sphere of preaching. How often some of us have labored to make the Gospel simple: and what an endless pity it is that we do not leave such work to the Holy Ghost! I sometimes feel that in our passionate desire to make God's word plain we may be thwarting the Divine purpose and hindering the Divine activity. When the Holy Spirit equips a preacher, He gives him words; while the preacher who is responsive, utters the word, the Spirit makes it plain. That is what Paul meant when he said that he had not come to the Corinthians with enticing words of man's wisdom, but with the story of the Cross, made clear, real, and forceful, by the Spirit of God Himself.

For a moment let us look more closely at the twofold nature of the Spirit's sphere. What He is doing in the Church we have already seen in the reference which has been made to John xiv. 16—He is the Comforter. If we turn to chapter xvi. 13, 14, we get a very important statement.

> "Howbeit when He, the Spirit of truth, is come, He shall guide you into all the truth: for He shall not speak from Himself."—*What wonderful words concerning the Spirit of God!*—"but what things soever He shall hear, these shall He speak: and He shall declare unto you the things that are to come."

The next verse declares the work of the Spirit in the Church—

> "He shall glorify Me: for He shall take of Mine, and shall declare it unto you."

Beloved, how much do *you* know of Jesus Christ—how much of the beauty of His character, of the tenderness of His love, of the majesty of His person? All that you have learned concerning Christ, you know only by the teaching of the Spirit of God. No man can call Him Lord save by the Spirit; and no man can know Him save by the Spirit. The first work of the Holy Ghost, then, is to make Christ to the believing heart

> "——a living, bright reality,
> More dear, more intimately nigh
> Than e'en the sweetest earthly tie."

That being the work of the Spirit in the believer, truth becomes to us, not a commodity to be stored, but a great sanctifying, purifying force in our lives. When the Spirit of God comes to the soul and says "Jesus is Lord," the soul responds "Jesus is Lord." It is not that the soul has found out a secret, but rather that it has passed into a new realm of life; and the whole of its being goes down before the Lordship of Jesus thus revealed. So, from then until now, the Spirit has been revealing Christ and reproducing Him within the characters and lives of the members of the Church.

Is that all of His work? Nay; look again

at John xvi. 8–11. Here you have the larger outlook upon the Spirit's operations. Jesus says:

> "And He, when He is come, will convict the world in respect of sin, and of righteousness, and of judgment"—NOT "*to come.*"

If I can impress that upon you, it will be something done. That passage is continually being misquoted, by the addition of the words "to come." The force of the statement may be gathered from our Lord's own explanation:

> "Of sin, because they believe not on Me; of righteousness, because I go to the Father; of judgment, because the prince of this world hath been judged"—NOT "*shall be.*"

It is not of judgment to come, but of judgment past, that the Spirit is to convict the world.

The work of the Spirit in the world, as distinct from the Church, is that of bringing men into direct contact with Christ in these three particulars.

i. *Sin.* Because He is the Saviour from sin, refusal to believe in Him is the specific sin which lies at the root of all others.

By belief I do not mean an intellectual assent to the historic statements concerning Him, but the surrender of the whole being to Him in perfect confidence. Unbelief, then, is the attitude of life unsurrendered and disobedient.

The Dispensation of the Spirit 45

ii. *Righteousness.* Because He has ascended to the Father, righteousness is now possible to all who believe in Him. Thus belief is not only for the putting away of sin, it is also for the bringing in of righteousness.

iii. *Judgment.* He has judged the prince of the world, and henceforth all who believe in Him share His triumph over evil.

The great enemy of the race has been bruised by the Saviour of men.

The demonstration of these truths to men is the work of the Holy Spirit. How did you find your way to Jesus Christ? Using some sermon, tract, or other human instrumentality, the Spirit convicted you of sin, of righteousness, and of judgment accomplished by the Cross; and you, through Christ, entered freely into the region of purity, power, and blessing.

In our present dispensation the Spirit of God is doing this twofold work; He is selecting—I use the word without a moment's hesitation, but you may use the word "electing" if you please—the members of the Church of Christ; but He is doing infinitely more. He is preparing the whole earth for the return of the King, as in every land He works through the disciples of Christ. He is thus undermining false religions and preparing the hearts of men.

Nations are getting ready for Christ. For example, the messengers of the Cross have influenced the great teaching centres of India, where thousands are flinging away false religions. Alas! that many such should be drifting into agnosticism and atheism. We can almost hear the footfall of the King as He comes to bring in all the wondrous dispensation which is to succeed this present preparatory one. Look where you will, and you find triumphs of the Cross by the power of the Spirit's work, and there are signs of readiness on every hand for the dawn of the day of God and the advent of the King.

Let us remember, then, that the twofold work of the Spirit is to make Jesus real to this age. He does this in the Church, by revealing Christ increasingly, growingly, progressively to believers, that they may be transformed into Christ's likeness. He does it in the world, by preparing everywhere for the return of the King.

IV

The Coming of Christ

I woke, and the night was passing,
   And over the hills there shone
A star all alone in its beauty
   When the other stars were gone—

For a glory was filling the heavens
   That came before the day,
And the gloom and the stars together
   Faded and passed away.

Only the star of the morning
   Glowed in the crimson sky—
It was like a clear voice singing,
   "Rejoice! for the Sun is nigh!"

O children! a Star is shining
   Into the hearts of men—
It is Christ with a voice of singing,
   "Rejoice! for I come again!

"For the long, long night is passing,
   And there cometh the golden day;
I come to My own who love Me,
   To take them all away.

"It may be to-day or to-morrow,
   Soon it will surely be;
Then past are the tears and the sorrow—
   Then Home forever with Me."
Hymns of T<small>ER</small> S<small>TEEGEN</small> and others.
"The Morning Star."

IV

THE COMING OF CHRIST

ALL Christian people are looking for the Millennium. It is an integral part of Christian teaching and of the living creed of the Church of Jesus Christ, that

> Jesus shall reign where'er the sun
> Doth his successive journeys run.

There is no difference of opinion among evangelical Christians concerning the certainty of that great future event which constitutes the hope of the world as well as of the Church. There are varying views as to how the Millennium will be ushered in; as to how the state of blessedness, foretold by prophets, and distinctly taught by the teachers of the new dispensation, will be brought about. All Christian people believe in the second advent of Jesus Christ, but differ concerning the time of His coming, the conditions under which He will appear, and the purpose of that advent. Probably the most popular view in current theology is, that the Gospel will be carried by missionaries of the Cross into land after land, until not only all peoples have heard the glad tidings, but, by the preaching thereof, have been brought into subjection to Jesus Christ. Those who hold this view necessarily believe that His advent will be post-millennial. Let me say, in passing, that this view of the coming of Christ is only two hundred years old, theologically; for, prior to the period indicated, it was the general belief of the Church that the Millennium would be ushered in by His advent.

We are, however, not particularly interested in theological views as held then or now; but we are intensely anxious to know what is the teaching of the New Testament about this most important subject. In the first place, then, let us examine Paul's first Letter to the Thessalonians, to which we must refer more than once:

> 1 Thess. i. 9, 10 : "For they themselves report concerning us what manner of entering in we had unto you; and how ye turned unto God from idols, to serve a living and true God, and to wait for His Son from heaven."

The words revealed the threefold attitude of every believer in Jesus Christ, in the early days of Christianity. There was, first of all, the turning to God from idols; next, the serving of the living God; and, third, the waiting for His Son from heaven. That was a declaration of the position of the believer with regard to the past, the present, and the future. He had turned from the idols of the past to God; in the then present days he was serving God; and to-morrow—the coming of the King! There was repentance, turning from idols to God; there was the consistent Christian walk through the days, serving the living God; but there was, above it all, shining upon it in beauty, the hope which maketh not ashamed—waiting for the Son from heaven.

Now, with regard to the first two of those three positions, thousands of God's people are fulfilling them, in the measure in which it is possible to do so when the third is forgotten or denied. There has been the turning from idols to God; there is the serving of the living God in daily walk; and yet, alas! alas! for years the Church has lost its hope, and has not been living as a people waiting for the coming of the Lord Jesus Christ.

If that be the Church's true attitude, the coming of Jesus Christ must necessarily be distinctly taught in the New Testament. I do not set any very particular value upon the figures which follow, but they are interesting for passing notice. In the New Testament there are no less than three hundred and eighteen distinct references to the coming of Jesus Christ. If you divide your New Testament into verses, one in twenty-five has to do with that blessed hope of the Church. And if you take these two letters to the Thessalonians—

the part of the New Testament which deals specifically with this great subject—one verse in four has a direct reference to the return of the Master.

Perhaps one of the most remarkable contributions, theologically, to the discussion of this whole subject in recent years—remarkable because of the source from which it has come—is the book which Professor Denney has written upon the epistles to the Thessalonians, in the Expositor's Bible Series. He has emphatically declared that the hope of the Church in those days was most unmistakably a hope that Jesus would soon come. He says, " It was this hope which more than anything gave its color to the primitive Christianity, its unworldliness, its moral intensity, its command of the future even in this life." And again, " That attitude of expectation is the bloom, as it were, of the Christian character. Without it, there is something lacking; the Christian who does not look upward and onward wants one mark of perfection."

I feel that something must here be said about the authority of the New Testament in this connection. I was speaking a little while ago, about this great subject of the return of the Lord, to a friend of mine, one who is in the ministry, a man of undoubted culture and also of spiritual devotion. He told me he thought

The Coming of Christ 53

it was a very beautiful dream, but only a dream. "Surely," said I, "you agree with me that it is taught in the pages of the New Testament: for instance, in Paul's letter to the Thessalonians." His reply was, "I fully grant you that when Paul wrote his letters to the Thessalonians he believed the next event of importance in the history of man would be the coming of Jesus Christ." I said to him, "What do you mean by saying that Paul *believed* it?" He replied, "If you read his letter to the Galatians, written at a much later period of his life, you will find that he makes no direct reference to this subject, and has evidently outgrown that early belief." That was to me an appalling position with regard to the inspiration of the New Testament. I said to my friend, "Then you believe that Paul's inspiration was nothing more than his own particular view of truth at a certain period in his life." "That is exactly what I believe." "Well," said I, "how do you know that, if Paul had lived ten years longer, he would not have outgrown his view of Christian liberty as declared in the letter to the Galatians?"

I submit that every epistle from the pen of Paul was called forth by the necessities of local circumstances. In writing to Thessalonica, he was seeking to correct those who had wrong views of the return of their Lord; while, in his epistle to Galatia, he dealt with Christian people who were becoming enslaved by Judaism. Every epistle had its specific bearing upon local conditions; and I absolutely deny that there was any growth, on the line of my friend's remarks, in the writings of the apostle. At the very last, when death seemed imminent, Paul still lived in the belief that his Master would come; and when he spoke ever and anon of the possibility of death, it was by no means a denial of his earlier position as manifested in his writings that the Church's hope is the coming of Jesus Christ.

The subject is so full and many-sided, one hardly knows which particular point to take in order to emphasize the fact that the next immediate event for which the Church (and the world, moreover) waits, is the return of the Lord Himself. May I ask you to read the seven parables contained in the Gospel of Matthew, chapter. xiii. They give us a sevenfold aspect of the Kingdom during this dispensation. What, then, is the general teaching of these parables? Do any or all of them imply that this dispensation is to be one in which the whole world shall be gathered into the Kingdom of God, by preaching? Careful examination affords evidence that such is not their teaching, whether we take them singly or collectively. The first four parables which deal with out-

The Coming of Christ

ward manifestations in this dispensation were spoken to the multitude, two being afterward explained to the disciples; the last three view things from a Divine standpoint, and can only be fully understood by those who are linked in life with the King, and so were spoken to the disciples alone.

Does the first parable, that of the sower, teach that, at the end of the age, all men everywhere shall be won to the Kingdom? Assuredly not. There is mixture of good and evil—some seed falling upon good ground, some upon secondary ground, and some upon utterly fruitless soil; so that there shall be a harvest reaped out of the world, rather than the whole world be won.

In the next parable, that of the wheat and the tares, the truth assumes another form. Here are two sowings going forward—not only the sowing of wheat, but that of tares by an enemy; and when the servants came and said to the Master, "Shall we root up the tares?" He replied, "No, let both grow together till the harvest." "The harvest is the end of the age," said Jesus to His disciples; "and at that time there shall be separation between wheat and tares." There is no teaching there that the sowing results in all wheat; but difference in kind, mixture, and final separation, are clearly marked.

Then there is the parable of the mustard seed which became a great tree. A tree, in Scripture, is always the figure of power. Nebuchadnezzar is spoken of under that similitude, and the king of Assyria, and Pharaoh; the great dynasties and forces of the earth are represented as trees. Our Lord simply teaches that Christendom shall become a great power and force—nothing more. I suggest, for your consideration, that the fowls of the air are emblems of evil and not of good; and that their lodging in the branches of the tree teaches the corruption of even Christendom itself.

Much stress is continually laid upon the parable of the leaven, as teaching that Christianity must gradually win the whole world to Christ. Is it probable that, when the Lord has already given utterance to three parables which distinctly teach mixture of good and evil, He should contradict the whole scheme of the first three by the fourth? The Kingdom of Heaven is not represented by leaven; we must have the whole picture if we would know what our Lord intended to teach. The woman who uses the leaven, the leaven itself, and the meal into which it is put—all the parts of the parable must be considered in order to a just view of its meaning. Leaven here, as everywhere else in Scripture, is a type not of good but of evil; and if you will carefully search your Bible, you

The Coming of Christ

will find that in no single instance is there variation from this principle. The symbolism of the Bible, from Genesis to Revelation, is never self-contradictory. If any have doubts as to the inspiration and authority of Scripture, they may find in what I have just said a point of profitable intellectual study. The symbolism of Scripture, with regard to color, numbers, figures of speech, in every case displays the closest harmony. In this particular case our Lord uses leaven as a type of evil. His picture is that of the manifestation of the Kingdom as being corrupted. With every desire to avoid fanciful interpretation, my own view of the case is that the woman who mixes the leaven with the meal represents the whole system of ecclesiasticism; and I believe it will be found that no part of the Church of Jesus Christ has escaped the corrupting and evil influence of that leaven. The master does not say, "Until the whole is corrupted, but until the whole is leavened"; and thus again you have the idea of mixture apart from the ultimate triumph of either good or evil.

Our Lord now turns from the crowd and speaks three parables to the disciples alone. First, a man finds treasure hidden in a field, and straightway sells all that he has, and buys the field that he may obtain the treasure. We will take the second of these parables in conjunction with the first; for it reveals the same aspect of truth. A merchantman seeking goodly pearls, finds one of great price, sells all that he has, and buys that pearl. These men of the parable are commonly regarded as types of the sinner seeking Christ. Indeed, one of our hymns runs:

> I've found the pearl of greatest price;
> My heart doth sing for joy.

Such an interpretation pre-supposes that a sinner can buy the field and the pearl; but this contradicts the whole scheme of redemption as made known in Jesus Christ. He who finds the treasure in the field, and discovers the pearl of great price, is Christ. How can I purchase Him, if He be the pearl and I the merchantman? What have I to sell which will procure for me any right or inheritance in the Son of God? Nothing, verily. He emptied Himself of His glory, made Himself of no reputation, and purchased us with His own blood. Ah! wonder of wonders, mysterious grace, only He can understand wherein the Church is His pearl of great price. I know nothing more calculated to humble us in the dust than His estimate of us; for, as we know and live near to Him, we are increasingly constrained to say that we are nothing worth. He graciously declares, however, that we are worthy the purchase of His precious blood. If that be the true interpretation, again we have selection from the dispensation. The buying of the field to possess the treasure, and the purchase of the pearl. He has not only bought the hidden treasure, but the field. The whole world is His by redemption price. His work is not ended in it and with it, when He has gathered out the hidden treasure. He has other things to say to the earth, other deeds to do, other victories to win; but the gathering out of the Church is the special work of this dispensation, as revealed in the parables we have just considered.

The last parable was spoken by Christ to His workers, who were to be like fishermen flinging a great net into the sea. Is the net designed to bring all fish into a state of goodness? No, it encloses both good and bad; then, at the end of the age, separation is to be made between the two. My sketch of these seven parables fails, because of its brevity to do justice to them; and they will well repay careful and prayerful consideration. The main thought, however, to be derived from them, and which I would fain impress upon God's people, is that our age does not issue in the conquest of the world for Christ; but in the gathering out of an elect remnant, leaving for a succeeding era another Divine work full of significance and blessedness. Bearing in mind the features indicated upon our Chart as characteristic of the present dispensation, a question of supreme interest arises. In an age of mixture, progressive selection, and ultimate separation, what is the next event for which we are to look? The return of the Lord Himself.

Let us rapidly trace the character of the age as revealed by various passages of Scripture. In 1 Cor. xi. 28, we have a phrase that bounds the Table of the Lord; and, as we sometimes sing,

> Thus that dark betrayal night,
> With the last advent we unite,
> By one blest chain of loving rite—
> *Until He come.*

The conflict of the Church and of the believer is to end at Christ's appearing, or epiphany, a word used only by Paul among New Testament writers—sometimes (as here) in reference to the coming of Christ *for* His people; at other times, in regard to His coming *with* them. How long is patience to have its perfect work? "Until the coming of the Lord" (Jas. v. 7). How long am I to serve in the King's will in this age? "Trade ye herewith till I come" (Luke xix. 13). When am I to be crowned? The apostle Paul says that he is to receive his crown at Christ's appearing—again using the word *Epiphany* (2 Tim. iv. 8). When shall we enjoy reunion with departed loved ones? When

The Coming of Christ

"the Lord Himself shall descend from heaven with a shout" (1 Thess. iv. 16, 17). Then it is that we are to be "together with them caught up in the clouds, to meet the Lord in the air: and so shall we ever be with the Lord." Whatever you think of as characteristic of Christian life and service in this age, you find to be bounded in the New Testament, never by death, always by the coming of our Lord Jesus Christ. Oh that believers had not lost their bright hope of the Lord's return, while they faithlessly and continually talk of death as their portion! True, we may "fall on sleep," and no man knoweth the hour of Christ's coming, save the Father; but the one bright hope of faithful Christian hearts is ever this—the Lord Himself shall come.

In his first epistle to the Thessalonians, Paul shows that there is a most distinct difference between the hope of the Church or the coming of Christ *for* His people, and the day of the Lord—His coming *with* them. The two things are clearly seen on our Chart, where the coming of the Lord is indicated by His descent from the heavens and the ascent of His people to meet Him in the air; but the apocalypse of Christ, or "day of the Lord," is marked by a second line which shows His coming to earth with His people.

> 1 Thess. iv. 16, 17 : "For the Lord Himself shall descend from heaven, with a shout, with the voice of the archangel, and with the trump of God : and the dead in Christ shall rise first : then we that are alive, that are left, shall together with them be caught up in the clouds, to meet the Lord in the air : and so shall we ever be with the Lord."

We need not pause; no one can possibly confound that statement with the thought of death —a thing which is there abolished. It is not death to which we are to go, but to the Lord Himself. The next chapter begins:

> "But concerning the times and the seasons, brethren, ye have no need that aught be written unto you. For yourselves know perfectly that the day of the Lord so cometh as a thief in the night."

Here is a very distinct difference between the "coming" and the "day" of Christ. The coming of Christ is His *parousia,* His presence; His coming in person into the midst of His people, that He may gather them to be with Himself. "But," says the apostle, "while ye comfort one another with these words, I need not write to *you* of the times and seasons. For ye know that the day of the Lord cometh as a thief in the night." The day of the Lord is, in one sense, begun by His coming; but it is a whole period which stretches out beyond that coming, the Millennium itself being included in the phrase. The context is against any supposition that the day of the Lord and the day of

The Coming of Christ

Judgment are periods of twenty-four hours. We know that the day of grace has extended over nearly nineteen hundred years; and the day of Judgment will last, at least, a thousand years. What we are waiting for, however, is—the King Himself.

After the resurrection the disciples asked Jesus, "Wilt Thou at this time restore again the kingdom to Israel?" and He replied, "It is not for you to know the times or the seasons." This expression, "times and seasons," is no haphazard one; but in the mouth of Jesus and from the pen of the apostle it refers to the whole providential arrangement marked out by God from beginning to end, and upon which this dispensation is an unmeasured interpolation—certainly, there is no measurement for the latter in Scripture. Continual pushing on and pulling back of dates has done more than anything else to bring this blessed truth into discredit. What, then, are we to do? Comfort one another with these words—the Lord Himself shall come. The duration of this age being known only to God, all His redeemed ones are to be ever living according to the Divine will, with their eye upon its consummation—the coming of the Master.

The people of Thessalonica misinterpreted Paul's first epistle, thinking that the day of Christ had come because they were in tribulation. Paul therefore wrote a second letter wherein he corrected this error, showing how that day must be preceded by certain signs, and that the Church waiting for her Lord, will not pass through the tribulation, but will be taken from the earth before it comes. In the opening verses of chapter ii. is a further wonderfully clear and concise distinction between the "coming" and the "day" of Christ. The words themselves are more important than anything which can be said about them:

> 2 Thess. ii. 1-4: "Now we beseech you, brethren, touching the coming of our Lord Jesus Christ, and our gathering together unto Him; to the end that ye be not quickly shaken from your mind, nor yet be troubled, either by spirit, or by word, or by epistle as from us, as that the day of the Lord is now present; let no man beguile you in any wise: for it will not be, except the falling away come first, and the man of sin be revealed, the son of perdition, he that opposeth and exalteth himself against all that is called God or that is worshipped; so that he sitteth in the temple of God, setting himself forth as God."

Before "that day" dawns, *the* final apostasy (the definite article is very distinct) is to be inaugurated by the revealing of the man of sin— not a system, but an individual. Paul tells us that this "mystery of lawlessness doth already work; only there is one that restraineth now until he be taken out of the way." Surely, to make Rome that restraining power would be setting Satan to cast out Satan, and evil to hinder evil. No; it is the Holy Spirit of God Who is restraining and checking the individualization of lawlessness. But when the Church shall be withdrawn from among men, the Holy Spirit will depart with it; for the Comforter, in accordance with the words of Jesus, abides with believers forever. Then shall the unchecked mystery of iniquity be manifested, and focused in one who will assume the very place of Christ in God's temple.

My aim has been to set forth Christ's coming to take His people away from the world, as the next event in history for which His Church should look. I stay but a moment to deal with a common misrepresentation of this truth. Some will say, "Then, God is beaten, inasmuch as comparatively few are being gathered into His Church." That is a very shortsighted view. God has never for a moment been defeated in the course of human history. Event has followed event in God's progressive work of redemption and regeneration, all the details of which have been necessary. The Millennium cannot be realized until the preparatory work of this dispensation has been accomplished; and this embraces not only the gathering out of the Church, but the preaching of the Gospel among all nations, and the undermining of all false institutions and evil systems of religion. Men may not realize that their passionate desire for the dawn of a golden age is excited by the preaching of the Gospel; but it is so nevertheless. All pure and holy ambition, as manifested in the attempts of thinkers to discover the secrets of true life, has sprung from the Gospel of the grace of God. The great words which to-day indicate the higher movements of the times, such as brotherhood, disarmament, socialism, solidarity, are the children of the living Word of God, the offspring of the *Logos*. Every gleam of light that is falling upon the darkness of men is a part of the essential Light.

> "They are but broken lights of Thee;
> And Thou, O Lord, art more than they."

All dreams of a golden age have their inspiration in the Gospel of the Kingdom.

In order that this longing of humanity may be satisfied, the Church must be taken away to allow of sin working out its full and most fearful manifestation. Then shall Christ appear with His people, to destroy antichrist by the brightness of His coming and to set up His golden reign upon the earth. No other outlook can be so full of roseate views and of hope for the Church and the world, as this triumph of God's rule and the accomplishment of His purposes in the way which He hath aforetime declared.

V

Daniel's Missing Week

"Lo, 'tis the heavenly army,
　　The Lord of Hosts attending:
　　　　'Tis He—the Lamb,
　　　　The great I AM,
　　With all His saints descending.
　To you, ye kings and nations,
　　Ye foes of Christ, assembling,
　　　　The host of light,
　　　　Prepared for fight,
　Come with the cup of trembling.

"Praise to the Lamb forever!
　　Bruised for our sin and gory,
　　　　Behold His brow,
　　　　Encircled now
　With all his crowns of glory—
　Beneath His feet reposing,
　　The whole redeemed creation
　　　　Are now at rest,
　　　　Forever blessed,
　And sing His great salvation."

　　　　　　　　　SIR E. DENNEY.

V

DANIEL'S MISSING WEEK

BETWEEN the coming of Christ for His people and His millennial reign there will be a short interval of seven years, full of interest because of the events transpiring upon the earth and in the heavens. On our Chart the interval as depicted does not show the correct proportion of time. The part with which we have been dealing is, as far as dates serve, drawn to scale; but this seven years' interval, if proportionately marked, would be hardly visible. The coming of Christ for His people concludes a dispensation, but it does not end His activities upon the earth. The period of selection and preparation closes, and the Day of Judgment and national dealing is ushered in.

In Matt. xii., from verse 18, we have a quotation of a prophecy concerning the Messiah:

> 'Behold, My Servant whom I have chosen;
> My Beloved in whom My soul is well pleased:
> I will put My Spirit upon Him,
> And He shall declare judgment to the Gentiles.
> He shall not strive, nor cry aloud;
> Neither shall any one hear His voice in the streets.''

I make a pause there of set purpose. What immediately follows is often quoted as if closely connected with the portion we have read; but it has nothing to do with the dispensation in which we live. "A bruised reed shall He not break, and smoking flax shall He not quench," is interpreted as if it referred to Christ's dealings now with men and women whose aspirations after Him are weak but will not be despised. I believe that to be an incorrect interpretation of the words, and ask you to notice particularly what is their real intention. There should be no stop save a comma at the word *quench*. Mark the construction,

> "A bruised reed shall He not break, and smoking flax shall He not quench, till He send forth judgment unto victory."

Then, there *is* to be a day when He will do such things; and in that verse you have another aspect of the work of Jesus Christ revealed. In the present day He does not strive nor cause His voice to be heard in the streets: neither will He break the bruised reed, nor quench the smoking flax, *till*—there is an emphasis on that word which we must regard if we are to understand the passage—"*till* He send forth judgment unto victory."

There is another dispensation of Christ's work in which He will do these very things. Some will say, "Surely there is no time coming when Christ will break and quench in such manner." No; not in the sense in which we have regarded the reed and the flax. We have misunderstood the words, in supposing that they apply to sinners weakly feeling after Him. The bruised reed refers to His enemies; the smoking flax to His opponents. In Isa. xlii. 1-4, you will find the original of the quotation: and the whole context there, as in Matthew, proves that "bruised reed" and "smoking flax" represent Christ's enemies, with magnificent satire in this description of them. What is a reed? Weakness. What is a bruised reed? Weakness weakened. What is flax? That which is easily destroyed. What is smoking flax? That which has within itself the elements of its own destruction. In His day of grace and mercy God will not break a bruised reed; it is bruised, and will be broken in due time. Neither will He, at this time, quench that which is already smouldering unto consuming. The great and beautiful truth which we have so often endeavored to enforce by those words abides; but we must be true to Scripture as it stands, and not attempt to enforce truth by misapplication thereof. In the time yet to come, beyond this day of grace and mercy, Christ will break and quench His enemies; and He will sweep before the majesty of His coming, as chaff of the threshing floor, the evil things which so affright us by their tremendous hold upon our age. In that day, yet to come, He will send forth judgment unto victory.

The same truth is taught in Luke iv. 18, 19. At the beginning of His ministry, in the Synagogue at Nazareth, our Lord read from the book of the prophet Isaiah words which revealed the scope and character of the dispensation that His first advent inaugurated:

"The Spirit of the Lord is upon Me,
 Because He anointed Me to preach good tidings to the
  poor:
 He hath sent Me to proclaim release to the captives,
 And recovering of sight to the blind,
 To set at liberty them that are bruised,
 To proclaim the acceptable year of the Lord."

Turn to the place from which the quotation comes, Isaiah lxi. 1, 2, and you find that the words, "And the day of vengeance of our God," were omitted from Christ's reading as recorded in Luke. Our translators have confined their punctuation to a comma at the end of the words, "the acceptable year of the Lord," and of course there was no stop corresponding to ours in the roll from which Jesus read; but at the point indicated, He ceased reading and closed the book. In publicly reading the words of a Hebrew prophet who hundreds of years before had foretold the coming of Christ, no one else would have ended there,

Daniel's Missing Week

for Messiah's work includes proclamation of God's day of vengeance. Christ's immediate purpose, however, was to indicate the first aspect of His mission, "the acceptable year of the Lord," as then beginning in Himself.

With equal certainty shall the Messiah once more take up that old-time prophecy, and fulfill it to the letter as regards "the day of vengeance of our God." The scriptures with which we have dealt reveal two aspects of Christ's work. "He shall not strive nor cry; neither shall any man hear His voice in the streets"—the story of His work to-day: "Till He send forth judgment unto victory"—the story of His work to-morrow. "The acceptable year of the Lord"—His work to-day; "The day of vengeance of our God"—His work to-morrow—beyond His coming to gather out His Church.

In popular conception the Day of Judgment is a period of twenty-four hours, in which men are gathered together to hear sentence pronounced upon them; but it is really as much a dispensation as is this day of grace. There is no reason to regard the one "day" as limited to the ordinary acceptation of the term any more than the other; indeed, such an interpretation robs the phrase of its majesty and beauty. What, think you, does the world wait for to-day? God's day of judgment. What do the oppressed masses need most? God's day of judgment. What is the groaning, sorrowing population of our earth asking for to-day? God's day of judgment. We shall deal more fully with the subject when we speak of the golden age in which the King Himself shall rule. This is the day of grace, and, at its close, the day of judgment will dawn, and will be characterized by the direct, positive government of the King Himself; but prior to His appearing with his people to enter upon that day, there will be the interval of which we must now more particularly speak.

Some of us still keep the book of Daniel in our Bibles, esteeming it as equal in Divine authority and profitable teaching with every other Scripture. Turn to chapter ix. The first two verses are introductory:

> "In the first year of Darius the son of Ahasuerus, of the seed of the Medes, which was made king over the realm of the Chaldeans; in the first year of his reign I Daniel understood by the books the number of the years, whereof the word of the Lord came to Jeremiah the prophet, for the accomplishing of the desolations of Jerusalem, even seventy years."

Verses 3 to 19 record Daniel's prayer of contrition and penitence concerning the sin of his people. In verses 20 to 23 we have an account of the appearance of the angel Gabriel to Daniel, bringing words from God regarding the future. Verse 24 contains a general statement:

Daniel's Missing Week 75

"*Seventy weeks* are decreed upon thy people and upon thy holy city, to finish transgression, and to make an end of sins, and to make reconciliation for iniquity, and to bring in everlasting righteousness, and to seal up vision and prophecy, and to anoint the Most Holy."

The Divine programme thus given to Daniel, as a representative of the Jewish nation, has a very obvious bearing upon our subject. We are familiar with the prophetic "week" as a period of seven years; therefore 490 years was the time assigned for the accomplishment of the prophecy. To say nothing of the interval between the delivery of this message and the crucifixion of our Lord, 1897 years have passed, and yet that programme is evidently not completed. But I ask you to consider a very remarkable set of figures in connection with this prophecy:

Verse 25.—"Know therefore and discern, that from the going forth of the commandment to restore and to build Jerusalem, unto the anointed One, the Prince, shall be seven weeks: and three-score and two weeks."

Now, what really happened? Exactly forty-nine years elapsed between the command to rebuild and the completion of the work by Nehemiah. There we have the seven "weeks." From the time when Nehemiah completed his commission to the death of Christ was exactly 434 years, or sixty-two weeks. Thus we have, in fulfillment of that prophecy, from the command for rebuilding Jerusalem to the Cross, exactly 483 years, as history testifies. What is left, as compared with verse 24? One week: that is to say, I have the account of sixty-nine "weeks" (the 483 years just mentioned), but the seventieth week is missing. Where is it?

My purpose is to show that the missing week comes at the end of the present age, an age which is an unmeasured interpolation upon God's times and seasons. As I have said before, prophetic truth has been much discredited by presumptuous attempts to fix a date for our Lord's return. Both Christ Himself (Acts i. 7) and His servant Paul (1 Thess. v. 1) have declared that it is not for us to know measurements which, in the wisdom of God, are not revealed. God will, in His renewed dealings with His earthly people, resume the "times and seasons" which were broken in upon when man rejected Christ.

Reverting to Dan. ix., let us look at verse 26.

"After the three-score and two weeks"—*see verse* 25 —" shall the anointed One be cut off:"

The Authorized Version adds "and not for Himself," a mis-translation which is corrected in the Revised, all Hebrew scholars agreeing that it should read, "and shall have nothing": that is, He shall not then possess the kingdom or be the acknowledged King, but shall be cast out. At that point in the verse comes a colon, and then we read,

> "And the people of the Prince that shall come shall destroy the city and the sanctuary; and his end shall be with a flood, and even unto the end shall be war; desolations are determined. And he shall make a firm covenant with many for one week."

From that colon to the first semicolon are words prophetic of the destruction of Jerusalem soon after the death of Messiah, not by the Prince, but by the people of the Prince. Then the prophecy passes on to events at the close of this age, when the Prince himself shall be manifested. The semicolon of Daniel is the comma which follows Isaiah's "acceptable year of the Lord." Here is the division between the dispensations; and at the close of the present age, when Jesus takes His Church to be with Himself, then "times and seasons" shall be resumed, Daniel's week (delayed, in the eternal counsels of God) shall run its course upon the earth, God shall accomplish His ancient purposes, and the prophecies spoken to His people in other dispensations shall be fulfilled to the letter. Signs of the times show that our unmeasured age is nearing its completion by the coming of the Master; but He teaches us to name no date.

Many among the people of God shrink from any reference to the book of Revelation; but therein we shall find Daniel's interval between the coming of Christ and the reign of Christ viewed from a new standpoint. When this neglected book *is* approached, the purpose seems too often to be that men may explain it away by reading into it metaphor, figure, and allegory:

> Rev. i. 3: "Blessed is he that readeth, and they that hear the words of the prophecy, and keep the things which are written therein."

The only book in the Bible that opens with a distinct blessing pronounced upon those who read its pages; and yet what part of the canon of Scripture is so neglected? Shall we not be among those who diligently, prayerfully, and humbly search what God would teach us in that last book of His Word? There is a key which must be used before we can understand what seems to be a labyrinth.

> Rev. i 19: "Write therefore the things which thou sawest, and the things which are, and the things which shall come to pass hereafter"—

the commission directly given to John, by Jesus Christ.

How shall the things mentioned be divided? "The things which thou sawest" are the visions of Jesus (chapter i.); and "the things which are" relate to visions of the churches (ii., iii.). Those letters of John were written to churches actually existing at the time, and the first application is to such communities; but the epistles reveal a sevenfold condition of Church life which is repeated with varying emphasis at one time or another in every successive age of the Church until to-day. They reveal progress, good or bad, in Church life and movement. We may find both Laodicean and Philadelphian churches now. "The things which are" exist in the present dispensation; but from chapter iv. to the end of the book, we have "the things which shall come to pass hereafter." It is to me, personally, a matter of surprise that the revisers have retained the word hereafter in i. 19, because the Greek words are "*meta tauta.*" The very first words of chapter iv. are "after these things," a phrase which excites little critical attention until it is compared with the Greek of i. 19. In both instances the words are "*meta tauta*," meaning "after these things"; and, as I have already intimated, the last section of the book extends from the beginning of chapter iv., where the door is opened in heaven, "after these things."

What, then, are "these things"? The dispensation of the Church upon earth, in its varied aspects. "After these things I saw, and behold a door opened *in heaven.*" From the beginning of iv. to the end of xix. a remarkable series of events follows on the earth. The Church of Jesus Christ is then in the heavens.

She is seen ever and anon in some place of heavenly glory; while upon the earth vials are being poured, trumpets are sounding.

Chapter xix., verses 11-15, give an account of the end of the interval with which this chapter deals:

> "And I saw the heaven opened; and behold, a white horse, and He that sat thereon, called Faithful and True; and in righteousness He doth judge and make war. And His eyes are a flame of fire, and upon His head are many diadems; and He hath a name written, which no one knoweth but He Himself. And He is arrayed in a garment sprinkled with blood: and His name is called the Word of God. And the armies which are in heaven followed Him upon white horses, clothed in fine linen, white and pure. And out of His mouth proceedeth a sharp sword, that with it He should smite the nations: and He shall rule them with a rod of iron; and He treadeth the winepress of the fierceness of the wrath of Almighty God."

He came to Bethlehem's manger to preach "the acceptable year of the Lord"; He will come with the armies of heaven, to proclaim "the day of vengeance of our God." He came long years ago, a lonely Man, our brother man; He did not cry nor lift up His voice in the streets; He will come again to break the bruised reed of iniquity, to quench the smoking flax of opposition. Another dispensation in the great plan of our King and Master will open when He comes to the earth with His gathered people,

VI

The Events of the Missing Week

. . . .
True is it that no heart may comprehend
   The glory God prepareth for His own,
And what will happen when this age shall end;
   But yet in vision Jesus hath made known
How fair and holy shall His Church descend,
   Lit up with light of precious jasper stone.

. . . .

And He shall make His Church all heavenly fair,
   With gold and pearls and every radiant stone,
And reign in Holiness and Glory there,
   And shine as suns and stars have never shone;
And He shall lead His Bride, His joy and care,
   With blissful singing to His Father's throne.

With eyes undimmed shall she her God behold,
   Behold Him face to face, and walk by sight,
Not trusting only, as in days of old,
   But seeing with her eyes eternal Light,
The great Salvation mystery shall unfold
   In that high vision of Love infinite.

                Hymns of TER STEEGEN and others.
                    "*The Blessed Hope.*"

VI

THE EVENTS OF THE MISSING WEEK

Our last chapter dealt with the "week" of years between the Parousia of Christ and His Apocalypse. Let us now consider the events of the interval, both on earth and in heaven. Fear and wonder will take possession of those who are left when our Lord comes for His Church. There will be on every hand strange questionings, producing conviction in thousands of souls, turning them, even during that terrible time, with their faces toward God. We might easily give free play to imagination concerning the effect produced upon those who remain. Fathers, mothers, sons, daughters, brothers, and sisters, will be missing, taken away to meet the Lord in the air; and the consternation ensuing may be readily pictured. Rev. John MacNeil of Australia, who has recently gone to his rest, has a very graphic passage in one of his books, describing this period when the taking away of a mother from her daughter may be instrumental in turning the latter from frivolous worldiness to the knowledge of God and the service of Christ.

But we are more interested in the effect produced upon the character of the age by taking from the world those who are found waiting for the coming of Christ. The influence of Christian character on the present age is revealed under the figures used by Christ Himself with regard to His people. He calls them the light of the world and the salt of the earth. Remove the light, and darkness ensues; take away the antiseptic, and there will be unlimited opportunity for extension of corruption and development of evil. The presence of godly men and women is to-day affecting the life of London to a larger extent than we think. We all feel that we are doing comparatively little for God in our great city. Doubtless I speak to many who have labored in London for more years than I have lived; but the twelve months spent here have burdened me with a conception of its need which by its vastness almost discourages effort. Still, the life of the great city *is* enormously influenced for good by its godly citizens.

The effect of the Church's removal must be twofold—many will turn to the Saviour; but, on the other hand, many will throw off the restraint which up to that time will have rested upon them. Corruption and evil of every kind will increase. It is in this way that the man of sin will be revealed.

Events of the Missing Week

2 Thess. ii. 7–10: "For the mystery of lawlessness doth already work; only there is one that restraineth now, until he be taken out of the way. And then shall be revealed the lawless one, . . . whose coming is according to the working of Satan with all power and signs and lying wonders, and with all deceit of unrighteousness for them that are perishing."

There may have been historic and local applications of these words, but it is the Holy Spirit Who hinders the full manifestation of that mystery; and the end of my quotation gives, in very solemn terms, the marks of the lawless one's coming and rule. Coincident with the Thessalonian prophecy are the words in Dan. xi. 36:

"And the king shall do according to his will; and he shall exalt himself, and magnify himself above every god, and shall speak marvellous things against the God of gods: and he shall prosper till the indignation be accomplished."

Now turn to 1 John ii. 18:

"Little children, it is the last hour: and as ye heard that antichrist cometh, even now have there arisen many antichrists; whereby we know that it is the last hour."

Verse 22.—"Who is the liar but he that denieth that Jesus is the Christ? This is the antichrist, even he that denieth the Father and the Son."

Chap. iv. 3: "Every spirit which confesseth not Jesus, is not of God: and this is the spirit of the antichrist, whereof ye have heard that it cometh; and now it is in the world already."

The spirit of antichrist is the mystery of lawlessness, the essential spirit of evil and of opposition to God; and it has been in the world from the moment of the Fall until now. The late F. W. Robertson, of Brighton, in one of his remarkable sermons, traces the diversity of manifestations which the spirit of antichrist has had in various ages, such as power, idolatry, or mammon; but it is ever the self-same attempt to underwork good by evil.

In that sense, the mystery of iniquity, the spirit of lawlessness, antichrist, is at work today; but when the Church is removed and the Spirit of God in His dispensational fullness is consequently taken away from the earth, there will be nothing to hinder the working of that Satanic power which will become concrete and incarnate in the person of one man. I have already referred in these addresses to a work which I recommend every one to read as being a most valuable contribution to the consideration of this whole subject, namely, Professor Denney's book, in the Expositor's Bible Series, upon Thessalonians. He emphasizes the fact that when Paul wrote to Thessalonica, he most certainly regarded antichrist as a person to be manifested at a given time. (With the Professor's explanation of Paul's intention we agree; from his interpretation of the fulfillment we differ.) This will be in the interval be-

Events of the Missing Week 87

tween the coming of Jesus *for* His people and His appearing *with* them.

Daniel ix.-xi. discovers a great world-power which arises during that period conquering the earth and entering into convenant with the Jews gathered into Jerusalem, in their unbelief; and it is a remarkable sign of the present times that there are now more Jews in Palestine, driven thither by persecution, than in the days of Nehemiah. In the midst of the seven years antichrist will break the covenant, cause sacrifice and oblation to cease; and a terrible period of suffering will follow—Jacob's day of trouble and calamity. Then, Dan. ix. 27:

> "Upon the wing of abominations shall come one that maketh desolate; and even unto the consummation, and that determined, shall wrath be poured out upon the desolator."

Here we have in an individual the most awful manifestation of evil the world has ever seen; one claiming to have Divine power and yet directly energized by Satan. During the latter part of the "week" will come the breaking of seals, sounding of trumpets, and pouring out of vials described in Revelation.

These seven years will see a marvellous gathering to God of stricken, smitten, and afflicted men. The hundred and forty-four thousand of the Jewish nation will be sealed; and the great multitude, which no man can number, out of every nation, shall be brought to Christ. Let us read John's account of this multitude in Rev. vii. 13-17:

> "And one of the elders answered, saying unto me, These which are arrayed in the white robes, who are they, and whence came they? And I say unto him, My Lord, thou knowest. And He said to me, These are they which come out"—

and here the Revised Version makes an essential correction, as compared with the Authorized, by using the definite article:

> "Of *the* great tribulation, and they washed their robes, and made them white in the blood of the Lamb. Therefore are they before the throne of God; and they serve Him day and night in His temple; and He that sitteth on the throne shall spread His tabernacle over them. They shall hunger no more, neither thirst any more; neither shall the sun strike upon them, nor any heat: for the Lamb which is in the midst of the throne shall be their shepherd, and shall guide them unto fountains of waters of life: and God shall wipe away every tear from their eyes."

We have been singing these words in our anthems, and continually reading them as if they applied to this dispensation; but it is only true in a general sense. Undoubtedly the Church shall have all tears wiped from her eyes; but the passage refers to the great company of those who come, not through trials such as yours and mine, but, by God's grace, out of *the* great tribulation which follows the taking away of the Church and the revealing of the man of sin.

How is this ingathering to be accomplished? I give you my answer with reserve, because many devout students of prophetic truth differ from me here. Personally, I am convinced that not all Christian people will be taken to be with Christ on His return, but only those who by the attitude of their lives are ready for His appearing. They who remain and pass through the tribulation will be awakened by the stupendous events of their times to the privilege and responsibility of witnessing for the truth in that age. Even in the day of Jewish sorrow God will dwell with His ancient people, who will then become heralds of the Cross; and under stress of plague, famine, and suffering beyond imagination, an innumerable multitude will "wash their robes and make them white in the blood of the Lamb." Those years will be such as the world has never seen —first, in regard to the manifestation of evil in forms more awful than we have ever known; and, secondly, in the marvellous crowding to Jesus Christ of a "great multitude which no man can number."

What of the Church during that time of tribulation? She is in the heavens with her Lord, all the retarding forces and probationary days of earth being ended; and Rev. iv. to xix.

gives a view to her position. During that interval the judgment-seat of Christ will be set up; and it is most important to distinguish between that, the *bema*, and the great white throne. The former is for the Church, and is set up directly she is taken from the earth; while the latter, which is an entirely different thing, comes after the Millennium.

> 2 Cor. v. 10, 11: "For we must all be made manifest before the judgment-seat of Christ; that each one may receive the things done in the body, according to what he hath done, whether it be good or bad. Knowing therefore the fear of the Lord, we persuade men, but we are made manifest unto God."

These words do not refer to the general Judgment. If you examine the beginnings of the epistles, you will find that in each case the writing is addressed to the saints, and it is of them the apostle speaks when he says, "*We* must all be made manifest before the judgment-seat of Christ." As sinners, our judgment was accomplished at the Cross of Christ, in view of which the Spirit convinces of judgment, not "to come," but past. To the *bema* of Christ, we His servants must come; and all our services will be tested by His eyes of fire. This need not affright, but should fill us with godly fear and heart-searching as to the kind of work we are doing for God.

"*We* must all be made manifest"; for God

does not dissociate our work from ourselves. Outward effort counts for nothing unless I am a Christ-soul; and then my life is my work. The question for each one should be, Of what sort is my life? If it is self-centred and unwatchful, so also is my work—"wood, hay, stubble" (1 Cor. iii. 12). But if my life is surrendered to the King, if I am loyal to Him and absolutely under His control, mine is King's work—"gold, silver, precious stones." I like to connect this scene at the *bema* of Christ with John's vision of the Master, in the book of Revelation, where He is pictured as with eyes of fiery flame. Here is a man whose whole *Christian* life of service has been "wood, hay, and stubble"; and the eye of fire consumes it. The man is saved, yet so as through fire. There is another whose work has been "gold, silver, and precious stones"; and the eye of the Master purifies it of dross, burns out evil, until the work sparkles with beauty even under the glance of the King Himself.

Then shall Christ's Church, not only redeemed but purified by the fire of His eye, be presented faultless, without spot, blemish, or wrinkle, in the white light of His Father's glory and holiness. Jude 24 and 25 describes this much better than any words of mine can possibly do.

> "Now unto Him that is able to guard you from stumbling," —*not falling*—" and to set you before the presence of His glory without blemish in exceeding joy, to the only God our Saviour, through Jesus Christ our Lord, be glory."

Rev. xix. 7, 8, gives what I believe to be the next event:

> "Let us rejoice and be exceeding glad, and let us give the glory unto Him: for the marriage of the Lamb is come, and His wife hath made herself ready. And it was given unto her that she should array herself in fine linen, bright and pure: for the fine linen is the righteous acts of the saints."

The dress of the Bride in this remarkable ceremony of eternal union with her Lord will be that which was purified in the fire at the judgment-seat. To this succeeds the apocalypse of Jesus, "Behold, He cometh *with* His saints." Thus we have traced the course of events upon the earth—the full manifestation of evil, the consequent sore tribulation, and a great gathering out of both Jew and Gentile; while in the heavens the Church has been brought to judgment, purified, presented to the Father, and eternally united to Jesus Christ. I hope it has been made clear that, during that period, the world is by no means God-forsaken. Every mundane event will be directly under Divine control; and through all the awful chaos, which will be far more terrible than anything hitherto known, God will be working toward the con-

Events of the Missing Week

summation—the coming of Jesus to set up His own reign.

I shall probably repeat again and again my personal conviction that ours is an unmeasured dispensation as far as man is concerned. "Times and seasons," which ended for awhile with the cutting off of Messiah, will be resumed when He takes away His Bride who is also rejected of men. While that is so, the signs of the times seem to indicate in the most definite manner that our age now nears its close. The general unrest plainly points to the coming of Jesus. Another portend is the return, long and distinctly foretold, of the Jew to Palestine, in a state of unbelief. Ritualism in all its varied forms is one of the surest signs of the end of this age. When the heart and spirit of true religion has gone, men ever attempt to replace it by outward show. The revival of sacerdotalism, the new assumptions of the Romish Church, and the Romanizing of the Anglican Church to so large an extent—(mourned by devout souls within her communion, quite as intensely as by those outside it)—all point to a consummation close at hand. Another proof that the coming of the Lord draweth nigh may be found in the fact that never has there been a time when all the forces of evil were allying themselves as they are to-day. The spirit of lawlessness is more and more throwing off restraint, raising its proud head, and laughing at the testimony of the living Church of Jesus Christ. To take one example—twenty years ago those who were fighting hard against the blighting drink traffic knew where to plant their blows; but it is no longer so. The action which turned breweries into limited liability companies has permitted the roots and ramifications of this giant evil to invade our churches until we do not know where the mischief ends. Without entering into party politics, we may see how banded iniquities contrive to win their own victories in elections, whichever side they may favor.

It is no less a sign of the times, that never was spirituality more marked in the Church of Jesus Christ than it is to-day; and to that blessed fact I bear testimony with fervent gladness. Everywhere, true men and women are hungering and thirsting after God, as never before. Let there be the spiritual declaration of the Kingdom of Jesus Christ and the purposes of God, and men are found eager to hear, learn, and obey. The great spiritual movements of the last twenty years—Keswick, Northfield, Southport, Star Hall, and the holiness movement of the Salvation Army—all prove that God is giving the promised latter rain, that the end of the age draws nigh, and that the King Himself will soon appear.

We stand, as did the men of old, in the valley, and ask the same question as they: "Watchman, what of the night?" Men of God upon the heights of vision, seers of the present day, looking out upon the great horizon, send back to us the old answer, "The morning cometh; the night also." The signs of the times are such as reveal the power of spirituality, side by side with the development of evil; but, thank God, beyond the night that comes is the larger day and gladder age for man.

VII

The Dawn of a Golden Age

The day of the Lord is at hand, at hand!
  Its storms roll up the sky;
The nations sleep starving on heaps of gold;
  All dreamers toss and sigh;
The night is darkest before the morn;
When the pain is sorest the child is born—
  And the Day of the Lord at hand.

. . . .

Gather you, gather you, hounds of Hell,
  Famine, and Plague, and War;
Idleness, Bigotry, Cant, and Misrule,
  Gather, and fall in the snare!
Hireling and Mammonite, Bigot and Knave,
Crawl to the battlefield, sneak to your grave,
  In the Day of the Lord at hand.

Who would sit down and sigh for a lost age of gold,
  While the Lord of all ages is here?
True hearts will leap up at the trumpet of God,
  And those who can suffer, can dare.
Each old age of gold was an iron age, too,
And the meekest of saints may find stern work to do,
  In the Day of the Lord at hand.

C. KINGSLEY.
"<i>The Day of the Lord.</i>"</div>

VII

THE DAWN OF A GOLDEN AGE

WHAT will be the condition of things upon the earth at the appearing of our Lord? The world will be groaning under the most awful despotism it has ever known; for the removal of the Church will have issued in the triumph of Gentile power centred in the antichrist, who shall exercise unparalleled rule over the nations, and who will then be at the zenith of his fame. Half-way through Daniel's missing week of years the man of sin will break his covenant with the unbelieving Jews, gathered in Jerusalem, who will become a persecuted, oppressed, and despised people. During this period, too, there is to be terrible martyrdom of those who, through the stress of the times, yield to the claims of Christ, as presented by His remaining witnesses. All the latest discoveries of science and the developments of earthly progress, so-called, will be pressed into the service of antichrist. Some of us have read certain books, the titles of which I cannot recall for the moment, in which the authors have allowed their fancy loose rein with regard to coming wars. I believe that in a popular periodical a story of this kind has been running, the writer working out in a speculative way what is likely to be the ultimate issue of the present arming of the nations and the endeavor to find new and improved methods for the expeditious slaughter of men. Think of the high efficiency attained upon the great continent of Europe in warlike machinery! In the writings referred to, there is, unconsciously it may be, an element of truth. The lawless one will avail himself of all the results of scientific research and invention, and Christ shall return with His saints to find the peoples of the earth crushed under the iron heel of an oppression far more terrible than all the previous experience can furnish, and exceeding the wildest flights of imagination.

In this connection we may refer again to the Scripture quoted in a former section of these studies—2 Thess. ii. 7, 8:

"For the mystery of lawlessness doth already work; only there is one that restraineth now, until He be taken out of the way. And then shall be revealed the lawless one, whom the Lord Jesus shall slay with the breath of His mouth, and bring to nought by the manifestation of His coming."

That is to say, by the epiphany of His Parousia, or the brightness of His presence. It is not that such destruction comes by Christ's Parousia, as the appearing to His people is called, but by that stage of His coming elsewhere

The Dawn of a Golden Age

spoken of as His Apocalypse or Manifestation. Among the old prophetical writings, Zech. xiv. 1-5 exactly foretells the same event.

> "Behold, a day of the Lord cometh, when thy spoil shall be divided in the midst of thee. For I will gather all nations against Jerusalem to battle; and the city shall be taken, and the houses rifled, and the women ravished; and half of the city shall go forth into captivity, and the residue of the people shall not be cut off from the city. Then shall the Lord go forth, and fight against those nations, as when He fought in the day of battle. And His feet shall stand in that day upon the mount of Olives, which is before Jerusalem on the east, and the mount of Olives shall cleave in the midst thereof toward the east and toward the west, and there shall be a very great valley; and half of the mountain shall remove toward the north, and half of it toward the south. And ye shall flee by the valley of my mountains; for the valley of the mountains shall reach unto Azel: yea, ye shall flee, like as ye fled from before the earthquake in the days of Uzziah king of Judah: and the Lord my God shall come, and all the holy ones with thee."

That is an Old Testament prophecy of this Apocalypse of the Lord with His holy ones; and now we may turn to a New Testament prediction, part of which has several times engaged our attention.

> Rev. xix. 11—xx. 4: "And I saw the heaven opened; and behold, a white horse, and He that sat thereon, called Faithful and True; and in righteousness He doth judge and make war. And His eyes are a flame of fire, and upon His head are many diadems; and He

hath a name written, which no one knoweth but He Himself. And He is arrayed in a garment sprinkled with blood: and His name is called The Word of God. And the armies which are in heaven followed Him upon white horses, clothed in fine linen, white and pure. And out of His mouth proceedeth a sharp sword, that with it He should smite the nations: and He shall rule them with a rod of iron: and He treadeth the winepress of the fierceness of the wrath of Almighty God. And He hath on His garment and on His thigh a name written, KING OF KINGS, AND LORD OF LORDS.

"And I saw an angel standing in the sun; and he cried with a loud voice, saying to all the birds that fly in mid heaven, Come and be gathered together unto the great supper of God; that ye may eat the flesh of kings, and the flesh of captains, and the flesh of mighty men, and the flesh of horses and of them that sit thereon, and the flesh of all men, both free and bond, and small and great.

"And I saw the beast, and the kings of the earth, and their armies, gathered together to make war against Him that sat upon the horse, and against His army. And the beast was taken, and with him the false prophet that wrought the signs in his sight, wherewith he deceived them that had received the mark of the beast, and them that worshipped his image: they twain were cast alive into the lake of fire that burneth with brimstone: and the rest were killed with the sword of Him that sat upon the horse, even the sword which came forth out of His mouth: and all the birds were filled with their flesh.

"And I saw an angel coming down out of heaven, having the key of the abyss and a great chain in his hand. And he laid hold on the dragon, the old serpent, which is the Devil and Satan "—*the name is repeated and given in varied form that there may be no mis-*

The Dawn of a Golden Age 103

take—"and bound him for a thousand years, and cast him into the abyss, and shut it, and sealed it over him, that he should deceive the nations no more, until the thousand years should be finished: after this he must be loosed for a little time.

"And I saw thrones, and they sat upon them, and judgment was given unto them: and I saw the souls of them that had been beheaded for the testimony of Jesus, and for the word of God, and such as worshipped not the beast, neither his image, and received not the mark upon their forehead and upon their hand; and they lived, and reigned with Christ a thousand years."

I have quoted that long passage of Scripture because I believe the Word of God, if we will but read it with simplicity, is more clear and powerful than anything that can be said about it. In the zenith of the power of antichrist, Jesus will be revealed from heaven with the whole company of His saints, coming to set up His own blessed reign upon the earth. His appearing will be the destruction of the man of sin, and the confusion of the confederacy of the nations against God and His Christ. He will scatter before His coming the evil which has been brought to so prominent a head during the period of that missing "week."

That will be the day of Christ's vindication before all the earth, when "every eye shall see Him, and they which pierced Him; and all the tribes of the earth shall mourn over Him" (Rev. i. 7). The Master has been hidden now for nineteen hundred years; and the scoffing world says, "Where is the promise of His coming?" Men are asking us if we really still believe in Christ as we used to do. Alas! that the infidelity of the ungodly should have crept into the very Church itself; so that there are not wanting those who have tried to undermine our holy faith, by seeking to rob it of everything that is supernatural and beyond explanation by laws which men think they understand. But as surely as God is upon His throne, Jesus, "this same Jesus," the Man of Nazareth and Capernaum, the Man of the city and of the village, He Whom crowds heard speak in the olden days, is coming back to our earth, accompanied by His saints. Christ's people also shall be vindicated when it is seen that "the foolish things, the weak things, and the things which are not," in the estimation of earth to-day, will prove to be things of wisdom, things of strength, and things that are. Then, too, shall the earth have its opportunity as never before.

May I warn you against spiritualizing this truth? Christ will indeed be the King of kings upon this earth. He will be as directly and positively a Ruler as any monarch whose name is upon our lips to-day; but His sway will be more absolute and powerful. With all my heart and soul I believe that the only

The Dawn of a Golden Age

effective rule for humanity is an absolute monarchy; but the trouble is, that we have never yet found the monarch. For a little while the heavens have received Christ, the only One worthy of unlimited rule; but the King of men is coming back, in infinite compassion for the world which drove Him out. For His coming, not only the Church, but the whole creation waits. The Revised Version gives a far wider meaning and greater force than does the Authorized to Paul's words in Rom. viii. 19, " The earnest expectation of the *creation* waiteth for the revealing [the Apocalypse or revelation] of the sons of God." To-day the sons of God, as such, are unknown, or despised and persecuted; but when the Master comes, they will be revealed with Him—and it is for this consummation that the earth is waiting. When He comes to set up His Kingdom and to judge, not with the hearing of the ear or the seeing of the eye, but with righteous judgment, then what solution of problems, what healing of wounds, what blessing for poor, oppressed humanity!

Following upon the end of Gentile power and policy, in the destruction of the man of sin, and the sweeping away of all war by the great battle of Armageddon, comes the restoration of God's ancient people of Israel to their true position among the nations. I do not say the restoration of the Jew—that is not comprehensive enough; but of the whole Israel of God. The ten tribes, lost for centuries, shall be found and restored to their land, for the fulfillment of God's purposes for Israel, and through Israel, for the race. I know that some doubt this truth, and say that Israel as a nation has been finally cast off. Can God desert those to whom He has made oath? Absolutely impossible! Can He be defeated? Never! God's purposes may be thwarted and hindered; but, despite all human failure and folly, they must eventually be realized. The prophecies of the Old Testament concerning God's ancient people have never been wholly fulfilled; and it cannot be that the inspired Word of the living God should prove a failure.

Deut. vi. 4, 5, has a direct bearing on this subject.

> "Hear, O Israel: the Lord our God is one Lord: and thou shalt love the Lord thy God with all thine heart, and with all thy soul, and with all thy might."

That is the Divine purpose for Israel. The unity of God is a great abiding fact, there coupled with heart and soul love for Him on the part of *the nation*. Connect with that passage Isa. xliii. 12, 13:

> "I have declared, and I have saved, and I have showed, and there was no strange god among you:

The Dawn of a Golden Age 107

therefore ye are My witnesses, saith the Lord, and I am God. Yea, since the day was I am He; and there is none that can deliver out of My hand: I will work, and who shall let it?"

Israel is God's chosen nation for manifesting Him to the world, and that revelation is to be made by their own loyalty to Him, and by their absolute freedom from the corrupting practices which have obtained among other people. Such an ideal has never yet been fully carried into practical effect; but because it is Divine, it has yet to be realized.

Before suggesting to you a few principles of interpretation for distinguishing the Bible prophecies concerning Israel which have not yet been realized, I ask, Are such predictions to be fulfilled? If not, we are driven into one of two positions. Either they are not inspired, or, being inspired, God has made a mistake. I decline to adopt either alternative. I have given up reading any book outside the Bible for proof of its inspiration. This blessed Book is gripping my inner consciousness more and more, and is compelling my obeisance to what must indeed *be* (and not merely *contain*) the very Word of God. The second alternative being obviously untenable, it follows that the prophecies are intended to be fulfilled. The distinguishing principles suggested, then, are as follows:—

i. Prophecies speaking of God's Israel as a whole, in fullness of blessing, are yet future. All the glorious predictions concerning the triumph and magnificence of Israel, are unfulfilled. They must and will be realized to the letter.

ii. References not merely to the restoration of the nation, but to its conversion, are to a state of things not yet realized, because God's ancient people are not yet regenerate in heart and life. They will be when they acknowledge Him as Saviour and as King, Whom to-day they are rejecting.

iii. When the prophecy speaks of Israel as restored to wander no more, it refers to the future.

iv. Descriptions of the utter and final overthrow of Israel's enemies are unfulfilled.

v. When the coming of Messiah is connected with national deliverance, the prophecy is unfulfilled. To some of us it is remarkable that the nation did not understand its own prophets. How did a devout Jew of the olden times read Isa. liii., with its picture of the suffering One? Well, he passed it over because he did not understand it, after the manner of many Christians in our own day, in regard to other matters in the Book, touching Israel's future glory and government. Part of Jewish prophecy has been fulfilled in the coming of the rejected

The Dawn of a Golden Age   109

One; but all predictions which connect His coming with national deliverance are still unfulfilled.

vi. When it is declared that Israel, as a whole, shall be a channel of blessing to all other nations, the prophecy is unfulfilled.

vii. When the prophecy was uttered after the return from Babylon, it remains to be fulfilled.

Take two instances in illustration. First, the beautiful passage in Isa. xlix. 18-22.

> "Lift up thine eyes round about, and behold: all these gather themselves together, and come to thee. As I live, saith the Lord, thou shalt surely clothe thee with them all as with an ornament, and gird thyself with them, like a bride. For, as for thy waste and thy desolate places and thy land that hath been destroyed, surely now shalt thou be too strait for the inhabitants, and they that swallowed thee up shall be far away. The children of thy bereavement [*the lost tribes*] shall yet say in thine ears, The place is too strait for me: give place to me that I may dwell. Then shalt thou say in thine heart, Who hath begotten me these, seeing I have been bereaved of my children, and am solitary, an exile, and wandering to and fro? and who hath brought up these? Behold, I was left alone; these, where were they?" [*Mark that question.*]
>
> "Thus saith the Lord God, Behold, I will lift up Mine hand to the nations, and set up My ensigns to the peoples: and they shall bring thy sons in their bosom, and thy daughters shall be carried upon their shoulders."

While I am not able positively to deny that

we, as a nation, are identical with the lost ten tribes, I am by no means satisfied of it; but I have no quarrel with those who hold that view. At all events, God knows where they are; and back to the old land for which He has declared His love, shall come the scattered earthly people—not the two tribes, not Judah alone, but all the Israel of God.

The second example is Zech. viii. 7, 8:

"Thus saith the Lord of Hosts: Behold, I will save My people from the east country, and from the west country: and I will bring them, and they shall dwell in the midst of Jerusalem; and they shall be My people, and I will be their God, in truth and in righteousness."

That is a prophecy never yet fulfilled; and I believe one of the very first things after the Apocalypse of Jesus with His saints, and when the man of sin has been destroyed, will be the gathering of God's ancient people to their own city. The consideration of God's purpose therein must be reserved for future study; but I may say here that the gathered ones will become the greatest missionaries the world has ever had. They will preach the everlasting gospel, and be God's messengers to other peoples, carrying all the truth of the Kingdom which they rejected when Christ came of old.

Rev. xx. 2, 3, shows that when the King comes and has destroyed the very incarnation

The Dawn of a Golden Age

of earthly evil, an angel from heaven will lay hold upon Satan and bind him for a thousand years, so that his deceiving of the nations shall cease during that period. Passing by, for the present, his subsequent loosing for a little season, it is one of the most glad and blessed prospects, that Christ is to inaugurate His reign upon the earth, by locking away from the nations the arch-enemy of the human race. Let me repeat that this coming of its King is earth's greatest hope. I have every confidence in the victory of righteousness, not on account of the organizations of the present day, but because I have faith in God and in the consummation of His purposes, by this coming of Christ to set up His reign among men.

> Surely He cometh, and a thousand voices
>   Call to the saints, and, to the deaf, are dumb;
> Surely He cometh, and the earth rejoices,
>   Glad in His coming, Who hath sworn, "I come."
> This hath He done, and shall we not adore Him?
>   This shall He do, and shall we yet despair?
> Come, let us quickly fling ourselves before Him;
>   Cast at His feet the burden of our care.

VIII

The Golden Age

Hail to the Lord's anointed;
 Great David's greater Son!
Hail, in the time appointed,
 His reign on earth begun!
He comes to break oppression,
 To set the captive free,
To take away transgression,
 And rule in equity.

He comes with succor speedy
 To those that suffer wrong;
To help the poor and needy,
 And bid the weak be strong;
To give them songs for sighing,
 Their darkness turn to light,
Whose souls condemned and dying
 Were precious in His sight.

· · · · · · · ·

Arabia's desert ranger
 To Him shall bow the knee;
The Ethiopian stranger
 His glory come to see;
With offerings of devotion,
 Ships from the isles shall meet,
To pour the wealth of ocean
 In tribute at His feet.

Kings shall fall down before Him,
 And gold and incense bring;
All nations shall adore Him,
 His praise all people sing:
For He shall have dominion
 O'er river, sea, and shore,
Far as the eagle's pinion
 Or dove's light wings can soar.

J. MONTGOMERY.

VIII

THE GOLDEN AGE

ANTICHRIST destroyed, Israel restored, and Satan bound—the personal reign of Christ will begin. Of that reign it is difficult to give anything approaching a full and direct description. A study of Old Testament prophecy may help Bible students to form some idea of the glories of that time. Let us look at a few of the chief features as thus revealed, considering first the Millennial order, and then taking some glimpses at the blessings resulting.

Jesus will be King, in as direct and positive a sense as any ruler the world has ever known, *but with larger empire and more autocratic sway*. He will be Judge as well as King, and the final Arbitrator in any disputes that may arise among men. In Luke i. 32, 33, we read:

> "He shall be great, and shall be called the Son of the Most High: and the Lord God shall give unto Him the throne of His father David: and He shall reign over the house of Jacob forever; and of His kingdom there shall be no end."

That announcement made to Mary concerning Jesus has never yet been fulfilled, but will be when the time comes for His personal reign.

He will be the King of God's ancient people gathered to Jerusalem; and, through them, the Governor of the whole earth. Psalm lxxii. has first application to King Solomon, but can only find lasting fulfillment in Jesus Christ. It opens with the words,

> Give the King Thy judgments, O God,
> And Thy righteousness unto the King's Son."

Then, in verses 8, 9 we have this prediction,

> "*He shall have dominion also from sea to sea,*
> *And from the River unto the ends of the earth.*
> They that dwell in the wilderness shall bow before him;
> And His enemies shall lick the dust."

In Zech. ix. 9 we read,

> "Rejoice greatly, O daughter of Zion; shout, O daughter of Jerusalem: behold, thy King cometh unto thee: He is just, and having salvation; lowly, and riding upon an ass, even upon a colt the foal of an ass."

The next verse contains a quotation from the Psalm just mentioned which confirms the application of that Psalm to Christ, because He has already literally fulfilled the foregoing words of Zechariah which speak of the mode of Christ's entry into Jerusalem.

> "And I will cut off the chariot from Ephraim, and the horse from Jerusalem, and the battle bow shall be cut off; and He shall speak peace unto the nations: *and His dominion shall be from sea to sea, and from the River to the ends of the earth.*"

The Golden Age

The remainder of the prophecy in that latter verse will be fulfilled in the Millennium.

Zechariah viii. 1–8 reveals the centre of government.

> "And the word of the Lord of Hosts came to me, saying, Thus saith the Lord of Hosts: I am jealous for Zion with great jealousy, and I am jealous for her with great fury. Thus saith the Lord: I am returned unto Zion, and will dwell in the midst of Jerusalem: and Jerusalem shall be called The city of truth; and the mountain of the Lord of Hosts The holy mountain. Thus saith the Lord of Hosts: There shall yet old men and old women dwell in the streets of Jerusalem, every man with his staff in his hand for very age. And the streets of the city shall be full of boys and girls playing in the streets thereof. Thus saith the Lord of Hosts: If it be marvellous in the eyes of the remnant of this people in those days, should it also be marvellous in Mine eyes? saith the Lord of Hosts. Thus saith the Lord of Hosts: Behold, I will save My people from the east country, and from the west country: and I will bring them, and they shall dwell in the midst of Jerusalem; and they shall be My people, and I will be their God, in truth and in righteousness."

Palestine, reinhabited by the nation of Israel, is to be redivided; and each tribe will return, not to the section of land previously occupied, but to a portion which stretches from the seaboard across the land. Jerusalem is to be rebuilt, and will possess a temple far larger and more magnificent than before, the size of which is given by Ezekiel. The city will not merely be the seat of rule exercised over Israel; but the metropolis of government for the whole earth, and the centre for the world-wide worship of God. In the past its sacrifices and oblations pointed on to Christ; but these, restored in the Millennium, will be offered in memory of the work which Jesus accomplished by His Cross. In Jerusalem Christ's laws and decisions are to be made and given; and from thence edicts will go forth affecting the whole of mankind.

All Gentile nations will come into a place of blessing as a result of this restored nationality of Israel. You will find promise of this in Gen. xxii. 18:

"And in thy seed shall all the nations of the earth be blessed."

That prophecy has never been realized, except, to some extent, in the first advent of Christ; but it awaits complete and very literal fulfillment in the age to come. The same truth is taught in Isa. lvi. 6, 7:

"Also the strangers, that join themselves to the Lord, to minister unto Him, and to love the name of the Lord, to be His servants, every one that keepeth the Sabbath from profaning it, and holdeth fast by My covenant; even them will I bring to My holy mountain, and make them joyful in My house of prayer; their burnt offerings and their sacrifices shall be accepted upon Mine altar: for Mine house shall be called an house of prayer for all peoples."

The Golden Age

As to the method of government, all the nations of the earth will be subdued to Christ's rule and will pay tribute to Jerusalem and to its King. It does not necessarily follow that they will all be loyal in heart. Sin will still be upon the earth, but held in repression, to be dealt with at the close of the Millennium. The great deceiver of the nations having been bound, and cast for a thousand years into the abyss, Christ will exercise autocratic rule through His chosen administrators: that is, through His ancient people, and, in some measure, through His heavenly people, the Church, who will be associated with Him in His reign over the earth. "Know ye not," says Paul, "that the saints shall judge the world?" (1 Cor. vi. 2).

Having thus briefly considered the Millennial order, let us endeavor to see some of its glorious advantages by reference to the visions of the prophets. Amid the groaning of oppressed men under the foolish and iniquitous forms of government which have blighted human life, how we long for a single Authority, just and final. That is exactly what the earth will have for a thousand years, when the One, rejected of old, is King in actuality.

The principles which will regulate government in that age are briefly and clearly stated in Isa. xi. 1-4:

120   God's Methods with Man

> "And there shall come forth a Shoot out of the stock of Jesse, and a Branch out of his roots shall bear fruit: and the Spirit of the Lord shall rest upon Him, the Spirit of wisdom and understanding, the Spirit of counsel and might, the Spirit of knowledge and of the fear of the Lord; and His delight shall be in the fear of the Lord : and He shall not judge after the sight of His eyes, neither reprove after the hearing of His ears: but with righteousness shall He judge the poor, and reprove with equity for the meek of the earth : and He shall smite the earth with the rod of His mouth, and with the breath of His lips shall He slay the wicked."

Then for the first time in the history of man, righteousness and judgment will be perfectly wedded. To-day the law, made for the sinner, too often hits the saint. Human judgment is always given upon evidence which results from a fallible seeing of the eye and hearing of the ear. But Christ, as an omniscient, as well as omnipotent Judge, will know the secret inward motives of the hearts of men. When cases are brought to Him by His administrators, His decision will, therefore, be perfect in equity. "With righteousness shall He judge the poor." He shall pronounce His sentence strictly on the basis of that intimate knowledge which cannot characterize the judgments of this age, under limited forms of government. We sometimes say oppressed nations need mercy and pity. Nay, it is rather strict, impartial judgment that is required. The most merciful thing in the economy of God is, that when His King comes to execute judgment and truth, the exercise of these attributes will be based upon His infinite, unmistakable knowledge of the hearts, thoughts, and intents of men.

Another phase of blessing is revealed in Rom. viii. 19-23:

> "For the earnest expectation of the creation waiteth for the revealing of the sons of God. For the creation was subjected to vanity, not of its own will, but by reason of Him who subjected it, in hope that the creation itself also shall be delivered from the bondage of corruption into the liberty of the glory of the children of God. For we know that the whole creation groaneth and travaileth in pain together until now. And not only so, but ourselves also, which have the first-fruits of the Spirit, even we ourselves groan within ourselves, waiting for our adoption, to wit, the redemption of our body."

Creation is to be freed from its groaning and travailing in pain; the blight upon nature will be removed; and a perfect manifestation of its beauty will take the place of all it now suffers in company with fallen humanity. Turning to Old Testament words on the subject, read Isa. xi. 6-9:

> "And the wolf shall dwell with the lamb, and the leopard shall lie down with the kid; and the calf and the young lion and the fatling together; and a little child shall lead them. And the cow and the bear shall feed; their young ones shall lie down together: and the lion shall eat straw like the ox. And the sucking

> child shall play on the hole of the asp, and the weaned child shall put his hand on the basilisk's den. They shall not hurt nor destroy in all My holy mountain: for the earth shall be full of the knowledge of the Lord, as the waters cover the sea."

You cannot spiritualize that passage. It is a plain statement of the fact that, under the sway of our Redeemer, the ferocity of wild beasts shall depart, and nature itself shall feel the blessed influence of the reigning Prince of Peace.

I have been asked whether the Golden Age will be marked by dietetic abstinence from flesh. While I do not believe in vegetarianism for to-day, except under certain conditions, I may express the belief that nature itself will then be free from everything which savors of cruelty; for, "they shall not hurt nor destroy in all My holy mountain." Certain it is that the lower animals will be vegetarians, for, "The lion shall eat straw like the ox."

I dare not linger upon these attractive pictures of nature restored, but must take them in rapid sequence.

> Isa. xxx. 24, 25: "The oxen likewise and the young asses that till the ground shall eat savory provender, which hath been winnowed with the shovel and with the fan. And there shall be upon every lofty mountain, and upon every high hill, rivers and streams of waters, in the day of the great slaughter, when the towers fall."

The Golden Age

Isa. xli. 18-20: "I will open rivers on the bare heights, and fountains in the midst of the valleys: I will make the wilderness a pool of water, and the dry land springs of water. I will plant in the wilderness the cedar, the acacia tree, and the myrtle, and the oil tree; I will set in the desert the fir tree, the pine, and the box tree together: that they may see, and know, and consider, and understand together, that the hand of the Lord hath done this, and the Holy One of Israel hath created it."

Isa. lxv. 25: "The wolf and the lamb shall feed together, and the lion shall eat straw like the ox: and dust shall be the serpent's meat. They shall not hurt nor destroy in all My holy mountain, saith the Lord."

These passages, taken almost at haphazard from among many, are predictions of what shall surely come to pass. When man, God's crowning work, first sinned, he dragged down all creation in his fall; but when Jesus shall come again, to reign in the power of His Cross, Passion, and Atonement (for that is to be the strength of His rule), then the whole creation shall feel the touch of His presence, and shall respond to His redemptive work. Ferocity shall be driven from the beasts, roses shall bloom in the desert; and the whole of nature which to-day is blighted and cursed by sin shall be perfected in beauty, because the King, Who has redeemed man and the earth, shall Himself be Governor.

What of man in that period of the Millennium? His physical being is to share in the general blessedness:

> Isa. lxv. 20: "There shall be no more thence an infant of days, nor an old man that hath not filled his days: for the child shall die an hundred years old, and the sinner being an hundred years old shall be accursed."

Premature death shall be unknown, and physical vitality shall be strong and generous. There are three verses which speak of the children under the reign of Jesus.

> Psa. lxxii. 4: "He shall judge the poor of the people,
> He shall save the children of the needy."
>
> Isa. xi. 8: "The sucking child shall play on the hole of the asp, and the weaned child shall put his hand on the basilisk's den."
>
> Zech. viii. 5: "And the streets of the city shall be full of boys and girls playing in the streets thereof."

What is the King's ideal for child-life? Play! With what shall they play? With that from which *to-day* we carefully and necessarily guard our little ones. "The weaned child shall put his hand on the basilisk's den"; while a little dimpled fist shall be entwined in the mane of the lion to lead about that royal playmate! What a glorious picture of child-life in the day of the Kingdom of Jesus Christ!

In Isa. lxv. 21, 22 we have a glimpse of millennial social conditions:

> "They shall build houses"—*well, that goes on now*—"and inhabit them." *The persons who do this to-day are few and far between.* "They shall plant vineyards,

and eat the fruit of them. They shall not build, and another inhabit; they shall not plant, and another eat: for as the days of a tree shall be the days of My people, and My chosen shall long enjoy the work of their hands."

It will be a great change; but when Jesus is King, profit shall go to the toilers.

There will also be unparalleled commercial activity:

> Zech. xiv. 20, 21: "In that day shall there be upon the bells of the horses, HOLY UNTO THE LORD; and the pots in the Lord's house shall be like the bowls before the altar. Yea, every pot in Jerusalem and in Judah shall be holy unto the Lord of Hosts: and all they that sacrifice shall come and take of them, and seethe therein: and in that day there shall be no more a Canaanite in the house of the Lord of Hosts."

The sanctuary will be free from the trafficker, and the trade of the nation will be characterized by being "Holy unto the Lord." Another note to the same effect is sounded in Ezek. xxxiv. 24–26:

> "And I the Lord will be their God, and my servant David prince among them; I the Lord have spoken it. And I will make with them a covenant of peace, and will cause evil beasts to cease out of the land"—*that is, men who prey upon the people shall then have no existence*—"and they shall dwell securely in the wilderness, and sleep in the woods. And I will make them and the places round about My hill a blessing; and I will cause the shower to come down in its season; there shall be showers of blessing."

See the security of life under the government of Jesus, when men sleep in the woods with no sense of dread. A closing glimpse comes through Amos ix. 11, 13, 14:

> "In that day will I raise up the tabernacle of David that is fallen, and close up the breaches thereof ; and I will raise up his ruins, and I will build it as in the days of old. . . . Behold, the days come, saith the Lord, that the plowman shall overtake the reaper, and the treader of grapes him that soweth seed ; and the mountains shall drop sweet wine, and all the hills shall melt. And I will bring again the captivity of My people Israel, and they shall build the waste cities, and inhabit them ; and they shall plant vineyards, and drink the wine thereof; they shall also make gardens, and eat the fruit of them."

A poetic description of the prosperity that shall attend man's labors in the coming days of the King.

I have found it increasingly difficult to confine myself to a comprehensive view of topics, any one of which might have occupied more than a whole chapter of this book. I have tried to give a general survey of the years when nature shall be freed from the curse; man realize full physical strength; profits go to the toilers; commerce be consecrated to God; men dwell in security; prosperity bring the plowman upon the heels of the reaper; and, above all, when missionary enterprise shall be at its highest and best—when God's ancient people shall go forth to all lands with the story of the Cross for the healing of the nations; when, hearing that story, men of distant lands shall take hold upon him that is a Jew, and shall say—"We will go with you, for we have heard that God is with you."

These glimpses of happy times to come require me to repeat that sin will not be exterminated during that period; but instead of being rampant, as it is to-day, daring to lift its head and laugh in the face of righteousness, it shall lick the dust and be kept in check by the presence of the Master. Then shall men know, as never before, the possibilities of humanity and of the earth under the righteous reign of God's own King.

In conclusion, it is always of practical value to know God's ways of dealing with men. If all this is to happen under the reign of Jesus by and by, surely those who have already crowned Him King may, even to-day, know something of the blessedness of the reign that is coming.

IX

After the Thousand Years

Crown Him with many crowns,
　　The Lamb upon His throne;
Hark! how the heavenly anthem drowns
　　All music but its own.
Awake, my soul, and sing
　　Of Him who died for thee,
And hail Him as thy chosen King
　　Through all eternity.

Crown Him, the Lord of Love!
　　Behold His hands and side;
Rich wounds, yet visible above
　　In beauty glorified:
No angel in the sky
　　Can fully bear that sight,
But downward bends his burning eye
　　At mysteries so bright.

Crown Him, the Lord of Peace!
　　Whose power a sceptre sways
From pole to pole—that wars may cease—
　　Absorbed in prayer and praise;
His reign shall know no end,
　　And round His piercèd feet
Fair flowers of Paradise extend
　　Their fragrance ever sweet.

Crown Him, the Lord of Heaven!
　　One with the Father known,
And the blest Spirit, through Him given,
　　From yonder glorious throne!
All hail! Redeemer, hail!
　　For Thou hast died for me;
Thy praise shall never, never fail
　　Throughout eternity.

　　　　　　　　　　M. BRIDGES.

IX

AFTER THE THOUSAND YEARS

A SCHOLARLY and lucid exposition of this subject is contained in a book written by Mr. George F. Trench; and from the name of that volume I have borrowed the title of the present chapter.

In the course of these studies we have dealt with seven dispensations of God; and we have seen that in the last of them, the Millennium, men will have in fullest measure all the things which have gone before: Conscience, History, Direct Divine Guidance, Law and Ritual, the presence of Jesus as King, and the Ministry of the Holy Spirit. To understand the events which succeed the thousand years nothing more is needed than an intelligent reading of plain and simple statements in the book of Revelation, commencing at xx. 7, and ending at xxii. 7:

> Rev. xx. 7-10: "And when the thousand years are finished, Satan shall be loosed out of his prison, and shall come forth to deceive the nations which are in the four corners of the earth, Gog and Magog, to gather them together to the war: the number of whom is as the sand of the sea. And they went up over the breadth of the earth, and compassed the camp of the saints about, and the beloved city: and fire came down

out of heaven, and devoured them. And the devil that deceived them was cast into the lake of fire and brimstone, where are also the beasts and the false prophet; and they shall be tormented day and night unto the ages of the ages " (*margin*).

We have seen that the Golden Age is to be characterized by the direct government of Christ. Sin will still be in the earth; but it will be held in repression and summarily punished as soon as manifested. The nations which Christ will rule with a rod of iron will be, to a large extent, disloyal in heart; so that when Satan is loosed for a little season he will straightway deceive them. True, there will be everywhere those who refuse enlistment under his banners; but the picture here is that of an enormous apostasy, the most fearful ever seen. The armies of the nations will gather together against Jerusalem. Not after the old fashion of patriarchal days will this warfare be waged; but express trains, ocean liners, and all the latest developments of science will be impressed for the service of the armies gathered from the four corners of the earth. There is no doubt that to some who have dreamed of the Millennium as a finality, the outlook afterward is disappointing; but ere the Kingdom of Jesus Christ in all its glory can be ushered in, the unbelief and disloyalty which lurk in the hearts of men must be brought to a final head.

After the Thousand Years 133

A study of the long list of apostasies—the Fall, the Flood, Babel, the Crucifixion of Christ, the Manifestation of antichrist, and this Revolt of the Nations under the personal leadership of the devil—opens before us an awful depth of human depravity, and should lead to heart-searching in the sight of God as to how far the elements of rebellion and sin still abide within us. A short, swift, burning sentence dismisses the rebellious host, "Fire came down out of heaven and devoured them."

The second stage of development which claims our attention is found recorded in Rev. xx. 11-15:

"I saw a great white throne, and Him that sat upon it, from Whose face the earth and the heaven fled away; and there was found no place for them. And I saw the dead, the great and the small, standing before the throne; and books were opened : and another book was opened, which is the book of life: and the dead were judged out of the things which were written in the books, according to their works. And the sea gave up the dead which were in it; and death and Hades gave up the dead which were in them : and they were judged every man according to their works. And death and Hades were cast into the lake of fire. This is the second death, even the lake of fire. And if any was not found written in the book of life, he was cast into the lake of fire."

What marvellous scenes are these, in the closing drama of evil! They reveal the last stages in its outworking and destruction. First, the rebel nations swept away; and then the dead, small and great, gathered before the throne. Can there be found in the whole realm of literature anything more striking than the description of that great Judgment day? A scholar, discussing the Book of God, as literature, said that while it is wonderful for its vivid imagination and magnificent conception, it is not equal in these respects to some of the old Greek writers. One present in the company where this was said, asked for an example from these writers; and the words were quoted from Homer—"Great Jove frowned, and half the sky was black." As against that sentence these words from the Apocalypse were given— "I saw a great white throne, and Him that sat upon it, *from Whose face the earth and the heaven fled away; and there was found no place for them.*" Surely from the standpoint of magnificent conception the inspired Word is far more wonderful than Homer.

In this scene notice that earth and heaven have fled away, and man is upheld in front of that throne by the omnipotence of God, and has no rock behind which to hide himself. In that final judgment of evil no man is rewarded because of his work. There *are* rewards for work; but they will be distributed elsewhere. The only escape from the doom of that day is a name written in the Book of Life; and those

After the Thousand Years

who possess that blessing are not present for judgment. Mark the clear distinction between the *books*, by the writing contained in which the dead are judged, and the *Book* of Life. Names entered in the latter are found there only by virtue of the atoning blood of Jesus Christ. Then are death, Hades, and all whose names are not written in the Book, cast into the lake of fire. That is the end of evil, and yet it is but the beginning of the glorious condition of humanity.

In Rev. xxi. 1 we have the third event after the thousand years:

"I saw a new heaven and a new earth: for the first heaven and the first earth are passed away; and the sea is no more."

The former heaven and earth have fled away from the face of Him Who sat upon the throne, for purification and reconstruction, not by water as at the Flood, but by fire. When the heavens and the earth, described by Peter as those "wherein dwelleth righteousness," are seen, the full purposes of God for humanity will be unfolded.

Next, we read of "the holy city, new Jerusalem, coming down out of heaven from God, made ready as a bride adorned for her husband." In verses 10-24 we have a wonderful description of that city; and any attempt to spiritualize it is out of harmony with the whole proper prophetic treatment of the book of Revelation. It is the city for which Abraham looked and for which we look; and it is not spiritual but material, as far as spiritualized people need material things. We may no more discuss this than the resurrected body of Jesus, which was palpable to the touch of Thomas, yet was spiritual enough to stand in the midst of His disciples without the opening of doors. The city's dimensions work out at fifteen hundred miles in width as well as in length, large enough to cover the whole of Europe. Making Jerusalem the centre, it would about cover the whole area promised to Abraham. I incline to the idea of a pyramidal rather than a cubiform elevation. Some regard the promise that death shall cease, as applying to the Millennium; whereas the old prophets tell us that in that period the sinner shall be accursed and the child shall die. But in this City of God, the great ultimate place of the Kingdom of the Christ, there shall be no death, pain, nor curse, because there is no sin.

"The nations shall walk amidst the light thereof" (ver. 24).

In that city, the earthly dwelling-place of a heavenly people, the old Jewish idea of Israel as betrothed and married to God, and the truth of the Church as the Bride of the Lamb, will

After the Thousand Years

each find fulfillment. Thus, our fifth point shows the kings and the nations of the earth in the light of the city, bringing into it all their glory and honor.

Now comes a verse (27) the beauty and value of which are too often obscured by hasty reading.

> "There shall in nowise enter into it anything unclean, or he that maketh an abomination and a lie."

It *does* teach that no unclean person and no liar shall be able to pass into the city; but that is the smallest part of its meaning. How came the mystery of sin into Eden? He who worketh abomination made a lie and tainted the brightness of the garden; and the stream of evil outworked into all human history. Into that fair city, Christ's all-glorious Bride, shall no unclean thing come. No temptation to sin shall ever be allowed to assault the dwellers in that home of the future. This truth reveals a Divine purpose more glorious even than the blessedness of the Millennium.

A seventh point of progression:

> Rev. xxii. 2: "On this side of the river and on that was the tree of life, bearing twelve manner of fruits, yielding its fruit every month: and the leaves of the tree were for the healing of the nations."

A difficulty seems to arise here in the sacred story. What can the nations need of healing

138 God's Methods with Man

in the perfect Kingdom, where sin shall be cast out? On the authority of a Greek scholar of repute we may substitute the word *health* for *healing*[1]—" The leaves of the tree were for the health of the nations." Healing pre-supposes disease, while health does not.

> Vers. 3 and 4: "And there shall be no curse any more: and the throne of God and of the Lamb shall be therein: and His servants shall do Him service; and they shall see His face; and His name shall be on their foreheads."

Remember that these are only passing glimpses of the glory of a kingdom on earth, *beyond* the Millennium, the great white throne, and the final casting-out of evil. This is a picture of the fullness of the times, when all things shall be subdued to the sway of Jesus.

There are passages in the Epistles which can only refer to this period. Heb. ii. 6-8 contains a quotation from Psalm viii., where four facts concerning man are stated:

i. "Thou madest Him a little lower than the angels."
ii. "Thou crownedst Him with glory and honor";
iii. "And didst set Him over the works of Thy hands."
iv. "Thou didst put all things in subjection under His feet."

[1] See "AFTER THE THOUSAND YEARS." By GEORGE F. TRENCH, B.A. (*London: Morgan & Scott*, 2s. 6d.) Footnote to p. 89.

After the Thousand Years 139

Reading further, we find Paul applying the fourfold statement to Jesus Christ. "What is man?" asks the psalmist; and, by inference, the reply affirms that there is no knowledge of man until we see Jesus. "We behold Him who hath been made a little lower than the angels"; so that the first of the four prophecies has been fulfilled: "Even Jesus, because of the suffering of death, crowned with glory and honor"; then the second is fulfilled. "But now we see not yet all things subjected to Him." Therefore the prophecy of that psalm, uttered before Christ came to earth, has only partially been fulfilled. In the Messianic dispensation Jesus was made a little lower than the angels, for the suffering of death. Here and now we see Him with His personal crown of glory and honor. In the period of Millennial splendor He shall be set over the works of God's hands. In the time beyond the Millennium *all things* will be subjected to Him.

There are three other passages in the writings of Paul, which have reference to this period:

Eph. i. 20-23: ". . . which He wrought in Christ, when He raised Him from the dead, and made Him to sit at His right hand in the heavenly places, far above all rule, and authority, and power, and dominion, and every name that is named, not only in this age, but also in that which is to come: and He put all things in subjection under His feet, and gave Him to be head over all things to the Church, which is His body, the fullness of Him that filleth all in all."

This purpose of God stands, though as yet it has not been fully realized, nor will it be during that Millennium in which hearts will be disloyal. It remains, therefore, to be fulfilled in the glorious Kingdom, beyond the destruction of evil and the great white throne.

In the same category is Phil. ii. 5–11 :

"Have this mind in you, which was also in Christ Jesus: Who, being in the form of God, counted it not a prize to be on an equality with God, but emptied Himself, taking the form of a servant, being made in the likeness of men ; and being found in fashion as a man, He humbled Himself, becoming obedient even unto death, yea, the death of the cross. Wherefore also God highly exalted Him, and gave unto Him the name which is above every name ; that in the name of Jesus every knee should bow, of things in heaven and things on earth and things under the earth, and that every tongue should confess that Jesus Christ is Lord, to the glory of God the Father."

That will never be until the Millennium is past and the great Kingdom comes which lies in the fullness of time beyond.

The last scripture in this connection is Col. i. 13–20 :

"Who delivered us out of the power of darkness, and translated us into the kingdom of the Son of His love." *The issues of that deliverance and translation may be traced in the succeeding verses.* "In Whom we have our redemption, the forgiveness of our sins : Who is the

After the Thousand Years

image of the invisible God, the firstborn of all creation; for in Him were all things created, in the heavens and upon the earth, things visible and things invisible, whether thrones or dominions or principalities or powers; all things have been created through Him, and unto Him ; and He is before all things, and in Him all things consist. And He is the Head of the Body, the Church: Who is the beginning, the firstborn from the dead; that in all things He might have the preëminence. For it was the good pleasure of the Father that in Him should all the fullness dwell ; and through Him to reconcile all things unto Himself, having made peace through the blood of His cross; through Him, I say, whether things upon the earth, or things in the heavens."

Jesus Christ will never be defeated. There is nothing of God's creation which will not be subjected to Him through Christ; no partial fulfillment of the words we have just read can satisfy the Divine heart. Not until Christ shall have banished evil, brought in the new heavens and the new earth, and given the City of God to the earth, will our Lord's work be complete and His glory at the highest.

Then shall come the time when Christ will hand over the Kingdom to the Father. When? I do not know. Mr. Trench expresses his belief that the period of the Kingdom will be far longer than the whole stream of time past, but acknowledges that nothing may be dogmatically stated on this point. Probably the glorious Kingdom of Jesus Christ, wherein all things are reconciled unto the Father by Him, will extend through ages of which we can have no conception. But there *is* an end, concerning which revelation was made to the apostle Paul; and apart from his words about this, we have no light upon the subject, as far as I know. He says,

> 1 Cor. xv. 24: "Then cometh the end, when He shall deliver up the kingdom to God, even the Father; when He shall have abolished all rule and all authority and power."

Christ will abolish these things, not merely in connection with evil, but absolutely. When He is supreme Monarch and there is no other power, friendly or hostile, in existence, then shall the Son also be subject to the Father, that God may be all in all.

Who shall tell the majesty and glory of God's purpose? Let us cease to have circumscribed ideas regarding God and His Christ. He to whom a thousand years are but as yesterday when it is past and as a watch in the night, is moving on, despite our fret and worry.

> "For I doubt not through the ages one increasing purpose runs,
> And the thoughts of men are widened with the process of the suns."

Who shall tell what lies beyond the handing of the Kingdom to God? Did you ever dream

After the Thousand Years 143

that there must come in the endless and illimitable time—which is not time, but eternity—a moment of weariness, a sense of monotony? Nay, think also of endless space. The sensitized film reveals stars which no astronomer has ever examined. Reach the furthest limit thus marked, and space is still before you. God is there, as here, limitless and unexhausted; and where He is, is love. All the things of which we have spoken are but the passing of His breath. While God and Love live on, there never can come weariness to the children of His love. "And every one that hath this hope set on Him, purifieth himself, as He is pure."

X

The Purifying Hope

I'm waiting for Thee, Lord,
　　The beauty to see, Lord;
I'm waiting for Thee, for Thy coming again.
　　Thou'rt gone over there, Lord,
　　A place to prepare, Lord;
Thy home I shall share at Thy coming again.

'Mid danger and fear, Lord,
　　I'm oft weary here, Lord,
The day must be near of Thy coming again:
　　'Tis all sunshine there, Lord,
　　No sighing nor care, Lord,
But glory so fair, at Thy coming again.

Whilst Thou art away, Lord,
　　I watch and I pray, Lord—
Oh, hasten the day of Thy coming again!
　　This is not my rest, Lord,
　　A pilgrim confess'd, Lord,
I wait to be blest, at Thy coming again.

Our loved ones before, Lord,
　　Their troubles are o'er, Lord,
I'll meet them once more at Thy coming again:
　　The blood was the sign, Lord,
　　That marked them as Thine, Lord,
And brightly they'll shine at Thy coming again.

E'en now let my ways, Lord,
　　Be bright with Thy praise, Lord,
For brief are the days ere Thy coming again:
　　I'm waiting for Thee, Lord,
　　Thy beauty to see, Lord,
No triumph for me like Thy coming again!

　　　　　　　　　　　　　ANONYMOUS.

X

THE PURIFYING HOPE

MANY persons will ask, What is the practical value of this teaching? The answer to that question is found in 1 John ii. 28 to iii. 3.

> "And now, my little children, abide in Him; that, if He shall be manifested, we may have boldness, and not be ashamed before Him at His coming. If ye know that He is righteous, ye know that every one also that doeth righteousness is begotten of Him. Behold, what manner of love the Father hath bestowed upon us, that we should be called children of God: and such we are. For this cause the world knoweth us not, because it knew Him not. Beloved, now are we children of God, and it is not yet made manifest what we shall be. We know that, if He shall be manifested, we shall be like Him; for we shall see Him even as He is. And every one that hath this hope set on Him purifieth himself, even as He is pure."

I fear that the question to which I have used these verses as a reply too often reveals the fact that the one asking has a wrong conception of the nature and value of truth. It is not a commodity to be stored, but a purifying and sanctifying force, bringing men into harmony with the will of God. The man who seeks mere possession of, apart from obedience to, truth, must fail in his quest. When God reveals Himself to man, obedience prepares for the reception of further and deeper revelations. In this connection we call to mind the declaration of our Lord, "The truth shall make you free"; and the words of His great intercessory prayer, "Sanctify them through Thy truth: Thy Word is truth." It is not a point of indifference as to whether any given view be correct or not. It is of the utmost importance that we devoutly, humbly, and yet earnestly, search out the will of God in the truth of God. What, then, is the particular value of the study of Bible teaching concerning things to come? John, who had such clear understanding of the affinity between Jesus and the believer, says that the hope of the Church is to be the reason for, and the power of, purity of individual life in its members.

The Greek word translated *hope* in the passage referred to undoubtedly has the same meaning as the Anglo-Saxon *hopa*. The word is often used in a light way which ignores its true meaning. Hope is a confident anticipation of good things to come, with corresponding effort to reach and attain them. It is not a mere consciousness in the mind, that something of value is to take place in the future. It is the setting of life and purpose toward that which the mind

The Purifying Hope 149

has come to understand and appreciate. The return of our Lord Jesus Christ is uniformly regarded by the apostles as the hope of the Church, though they may treat of it under varied aspects, such as the reward of workers, the destruction of evil, meeting with loved ones gone before, and the inexpressible delight of the Lord's presence. Let us examine a few of such passages:

(i.) Rom. viii. 17–25: "—— heirs of God, and joint-heirs with Christ; if so be that we suffer with Him, that we may be also glorified with Him. For I reckon that the sufferings of this present time are not worthy to be compared with the glory which shall be revealed to us-ward. For the earnest expectation of the creation waiteth for the revealing of the sons of God. For the creation was subjected to vanity, not of its own will, but by reason of Him who subjected it, in HOPE that the creation itself also shall be delivered from the bondage of corruption into the liberty of the glory of the children of God. For we know that the whole creation groaneth and travaileth in pain together until now. And not only so, but ourselves also, which have the first-fruits of the Spirit, even we ourselves groan within ourselves, waiting for our adoption, to wit, the redemption of our body. For by hope were we saved : but hope that is seen is not hope: for who hopeth for that which he seeth? But if we hope for that which we see not, then do we with patience wait for it."

Evidently, in the mind of the apostle, the completion of redemption—that is, the redemption of the body—is the hope of the Church.

(ii.) Titus ii. 11–13: "For the grace of God hath appeared, bringing salvation to all men, instructing us, to the intent that, denying ungodliness and worldly lusts, we should live soberly and righteously and godly in this present world; looking for the blessed HOPE and appearing of the glory of our great God and Saviour Jesus Christ."

In this case the apostle links the Church's hope with the epiphany of the glory.

(iii.) Heb. x. 19–23: "Having therefore, brethren, boldness to enter into the holy place by the blood of Jesus, by the way which He dedicated for us, a new and living way, through the veil, that is to say, His flesh; and having a great Priest over the house of God; let us draw near with a true heart in fullness of faith, having our hearts sprinkled from an evil conscience, and our body washed with pure water: let us hold fast the confession of our HOPE that it waver not; for He is faithful that promised."

The translation in the Authorized Version, "Let us hold fast the profession of our *faith*," is inexplicable, when the Greek word there used is rendered *hope* in every other New Testament passage. Faith has been mentioned in verse 22; and, in its fullness, we are to draw near into the holy place. It is the confession of our *hope* that we are to hold fast; and the nature of that hope is evident from verses 25 and 35–37:

"Not forsaking the assembling of ourselves together, as the custom of some is, but exhorting one another; and so much the more, as ye see the day drawing nigh.

The Purifying Hope 151

". . . Cast not away therefore your boldness, which hath great recompense of reward. For ye have need of patience, that, having done the will of God, ye may receive the promise. For yet a very little while, He that cometh shall come, and shall not tarry."

The coming of the Blessed One is the hope which we are to hold fast, as we come to God in fullness of faith.

(iv.) 1 Peter i. 3, 5: "Blessed be the God and Father of our Lord Jesus Christ, Who according to His great mercy begat us again unto a living HOPE by the resurrection of Jesus Christ from the dead, unto an inheritance incorruptible, and undefiled, and that fadeth not away, reserved in heaven for you, who by the power of God are guarded through faith unto a salvation ready to be revealed in the last time."

The hope of the Church is, in this aspect, a salvation to be revealed in all its fullness when Jesus Christ Himself shall come.

(v.) Reverting to the verses with which we started, in the words " He that hath this HOPE," the apostle of love refers to the day when we shall see Christ as He is, and be like Him. It is this hope toward which the Church looks with confidence and takes her way through days of patient waiting.

An alteration, apparently trivial, and yet of vital importance to a right estimate of this hope, is made in 1 John iii. 3. Instead of "*this hope in him*," as in the Authorized, we have "this hope set on Him," and the pronoun should have a capital letter, for it refers to Jesus Christ as the revelation of the Father. "Behold what manner of love the Father hath bestowed upon us, that we should be called children of God"; and the argument proceeds, from the Father through the Son, to the point of hope's purifying effect.

Then, this hope "maketh not ashamed." There is no uncertainty about it, and it cannot be hindered. That which has become the Church's beacon, casting a ray of glory upon her dark night, is no false light luring to destruction. This hope, being set upon God in His purpose and arrangement, and not upon our individual life, the circumstances of a day, the conditions of a century, or the changing policy of ecclesiasticism, is lifted clear away from the strife of party and from human uncertainty. As sure as God is, the hidden Man Christ Jesus, the King Whom the heavens have received for a season, must come again: and the light and the glory of that promise is the hope of the Church.

If it be indeed true that Jesus is coming; and if, in the wisdom of God, the date of His return has been absolutely hidden from man—how should we live as those to whom God has given that coming as the supreme and only hope of our life? The question answers itself.

This is a purifying hope, because it regulates

The Purifying Hope

the attitude of the believer's life toward Christ. Through all the passing years we are to wait for Him, expecting that at any moment, above the din and strife of earth, we may hear His call. There is no other *purifying* hope. I take it for granted that no true child of God cherishes the sordid ambitions of worldly men, such as the hope of wealth or of fame. Yet our *hope* may be set upon an opening for ourselves in the mission field or in the service of humanity at home. As long as hope is set upon service, it is not fixed upon Christ, and *He* should hold full and absolute possession of our hearts. Our lives may be so occupied with things good in themselves, that we do not see the King. In the will of God, however, there is but one attitude for the believer—that of the pilgrim, with loins girt and staff in hand, waiting for the break of day, the coming of the King. Do not misunderstand me. If we are truly waiting for Jesus, we shall not be careless of those for whom He died: and we shall not dare disobey His word which bids us preach the gospel to every creature. But, as far as individual life is concerned, the coming One should fill the heart's vision through all the days and moments.

How will this affect our behavior? I would suggest questions rather than attempt to answer them; for your own minds and hearts will be busy on this point. How should I transact my business, knowing that even as I make an entry in my ledger I may be interrupted by the call of my Master? How should I take my recreation when, at any moment, He may summon me from it to His own presence? The purifying effect of such considerations are evident. We are to serve our generation, live in our homes, do our business, and take our recreation, in readiness to leave all at any moment. Some one says, "That will make a very strained sort of life." I think not.

Mr. Wesley was once asked by a lady, "Suppose that you knew you were to die at twelve o'clock to-morrow night, how would you spend the intervening time?" "How, madam?" he replied; "why, just as I intend to spend it now. I should preach this night at Gloucester, and again at five to-morrow morning; after that I should ride to Tewkesbury, preach in the afternoon, and meet the societies in the evening. I should then repair to friend Martin's house, who expects to entertain me, converse and pray with the family as usual, retire to my room at ten o'clock, commend myself to my heavenly Father, lie down to rest, and wake up in glory."[1]

No man lived a more strong and beautiful life than did John Wesley, and his view of death

[1] "Anecdotes of the Wesleys."—WAKERLEY.

The Purifying Hope 155

was that whenever it came he would be found at his duty; and the transition from that duty to heaven's service would be a natural one. Instead of death, let the Lord be expected; and the true attitude of life will be that of quiet pursuit of duty and constant readiness to greet Him.

But you say to me, "Would you like Jesus to come and find you playing with your children?" Why not? I know of no occupation that I believe would be more pleasing to the heart of my King! It would be a proof of my belief in the blessedness of His reign, when the children are to have a perfect playtime.

When Jesus went from earth, the clouds at which His disciples gazed were riven, and an angel appeared, saying:

> "Why stand ye looking into heaven? This Jesus . . . shall so come in like manner as ye beheld Him going into heaven!"—

that is, in the clouds, not merely in a spiritual sense. Thus, at the earliest moment in the "little while," the attitude of star-gazing was rebuked; and His disciples were sent to the discharge of duty, to look for Him from the midst of loyal service. Alas! that some who profess to believe in the coming of the Lord, should give up all the things which they were intended to sanctify. We are to be busy about our appointed task; to influence our day and generation as far as in us lies, by a reproduction in the power of the Spirit of the pure character of Jesus Christ; and all the while to have a listening ear for the Master's call, and the longing to welcome Him when He comes.

This hope also lights up circumstances. Are you entrusted by God with the great responsibility of riches? Expecting the Lord's return, you will use that wealth for Him. Are your days filled with stress of poverty and necessity for careful planning in regard to means? In the light of that promise, even poverty is transfigured. I am not now discussing the great questions of poverty and wealth. I regard poverty as a curse! God never meant any one to be poor, in the sense of that pinching, grinding want, which gives a man heart-ache and brain-ache. There is plenty in the world for every man to live in comfort, and all lack is the result of human mismanagement. The light of that coming upon friendship forbids unholy alliances and ennobles sanctified comradeship; and when it falls upon the graves where our sacred dust rests, how beautiful they become! We shall meet in "the morning."

> "Some from earth, from glory some:
> Severed only till He come."

The bright rays of this truth shine for me upon some of the most perplexing problems of the Book of God and of the times in which we live. In my New Testament I find the free-will of man and the sovereignty of God both distinctly taught. These things were long a source of perplexity to me. The view which I strongly hold, that Christ is coming for His Church, an elect company out of the multitude of the saved, has solved for me a most difficult problem. I believe that Divine election has reference to membership in the Church of the Firstborn, not to personal salvation; and I believe, therefore, that there will be great multitudes saved by the finished work of Christ who are not members of that sacred body.

Christ's coming throws light upon other problems in the Book, in current theological thought, and in present-day life. How can we find comfort in missionary enterprise unless we believe in Christ's coming and the more blessed dispensation which lies beyond? Let the societies add to their statistics the facts that within a year the heathen have multiplied in a ratio far exceeding the number of converts made; and that the proportion of Christians to the mass of mankind is smaller to-day than it was fifty years ago. Where is your comfort, in view of these facts? Along such a vista of missionary work God appears as being beaten out of His own world! We believe that the King is doing work preparatory to His coming. He is gathering out His Church, and in a thousand ways making straight His paths by the proclamation of the Gospel in all lands, so that when the ancient people of God shall become His messengers to all peoples they will find a readiness to receive the message as the result. In this view we have hope for the nations of the earth and for the ages which lie ahead.

The light of this truth falls also upon the chaos and unrest of our age—arming of nations, mutual distrust, "wars, and rumors of wars." Man is failing in governmental power; and the hope of the world is that Jesus will come to rule within the lines of His own royal policy. Once take firm hold of this great truth of the coming of the King, and it affords a bright outlook along every avenue of life and brings gladness to the weary heart.

Our responsibility is marked in the passage to which I have more than once referred:

1 John ii. 28: "And now, my little children, abide in Him; that, if He shall be manifested, we may have boldness, and not be ashamed before Him at His coming."

The *if* casts no doubt upon His appearing, but is indicative of a coming at any time. An alternative possibility is here suggested as to the attitude of *Christians* at that coming. They may "have boldness" or "be ashamed."

With regard to the first: the word "*bold-*

The Purifying Hope 159

ness" (in place of confidence, A. V.), by no means conveys the whole force of the original. The idea is that we may have the freedom of speech which comes of the perfect familiarity of friendship. We all know how the diffidence and awkwardness which come of the sense of being out of place, paralyze speech. This, I imagine, would be the position of most of us if granted a personal interview with Queen Victoria. Not only should we be at a loss in regard to deportment, but we should wonder what to say, and be anxious as to whether we had said it aright or not. May God help us so to abide in Christ that when He comes we may not feel the awkwardness which arises from the constraint of being strangers to Him, but that we may be able to say—This is our Master, we have known him by faith and now we see Him. We have poured in to His listening ear the tale of our sorrows in the day of mystery and darkness, and now we may talk with Him face to face (see Isa. xxv. 9).

Mark the other possibility, ". . . and not be ashamed *from* Him at His coming" (the preposition is *apo*, away from). The picture is that of persons so conscious of unreadiness that they dare not face Him. The root meaning of the word *ashamed* is *disgraced*, so that it is allowable to read, " and not be disgraced from Him at His coming." This is not addressed to the outside world, but to the believer in Christ. In that verse there is a very clear division which, to my mind, answers the question whether believers may not pass through the great tribulation. Some will be ready to enjoy freedom of access to Christ and familiarity with Him; but the "little children" of God who have been living only in the elements of the world will be disgraced at His appearing.

What are we to do, as Christian men and women, in the light of these two possibilities? I give two passages from the Epistle, as my closing words: "My little children, abide in Him"; "Every one that hath this hope set on Him purifieth himself." Those who are abiding in Christ here on earth, who purify themselves as He is pure, separated ones cut clean adrift from the ungodliness of the age, loyal of heart to the King in the days of waiting for Him—these are the men and women who will have boldness in the day of His coming.

Who shall draw the line? I do not. It is for each of us to make application of this truth in solitude.

APPENDIX

"Come, Holy Ghost—for moved by Thee
    The prophets wrote and spoke—
Unlock the truth, Thyself the key:
    Unseal the sacred Book."

WESLEY.

APPENDIX

BEING AN ADDRESS GIVEN AT THE CLOSE OF THE SERIES IN ANSWER TO WRITTEN QUESTIONS SENT IN

THE interest taken in the important subject of God's dispensational dealings with man has been evidenced by the questions that have reached me in response to my invitation. I am very glad to say that, as far as one may judge from the tone of the writers, not a single query has been sent for the sake of controversy. Some friends have written differing from positions I have taken; and that was only to be anticipated. God's truth is too wonderful to be so formulated that it shall be intelligible in its entirety to every one. Thank God, however, it is our joyful hope that when the Lord doth bring again Zion, we shall see eye to eye.

The same question has come in varied forms from many persons. It has been no easy task to analyze and classify, as a necessary preliminary. No attempt has been made to deal with irrelevant questions bearing upon the wider field of prophecy, in topics not directly related to the exact line of study we have taken.

I have selected fourteen typical questions which call for answers of varying length in accordance with their relative importance.

1. *Is it not clear that half Daniel's missing week has already gone in the three-and-a-half years of our Lord's earthly ministry?*

Many hold that view; but, personally, I cannot do so, because of the clear and distinct division of the "weeks" in Dan. ix. 26, 27. "And after the three-score and two weeks shall the Anointed One be cut off, and shall have nothing." The Authorized Version says Messiah shall be "cut off, but not for Himself"—words which are certainly not justified by the original. The sense is that He shall be without dominion. "And the people of the prince that shall come shall destroy the city and the sanctuary": that is, the people who are guided by the same principle of government that eventually characterizes the rule of antichrist. This scripture, thus far, was undoubtedly fulfilled in the coming of the Roman legions and the destruction which came upon Jerusalem after the death of Christ. "And his end shall be with a flood, and even unto the end shall be war; desolations are determined. And he shall make a firm covenant with many for one week: and for the half of the week he shall cause the sacrifice and the oblation to cease,"

Appendix

The whole "week" lies in the future. The prince, or antichrist, is to make a covenant for a week which he will break in the midst of that period, and then will follow the half-week of terrible persecution and tribulation of which we have spoken at length. I have also dealt very fully with the seventy sevens of Daniel; and I therefore only touch upon them to say that they consist —

(i.) Of the forty-nine years which commenced with the permission given to Nehemiah to rebuild Jerusalem, and ended with the completing of the wall.

(ii.) Of the four hundred and thirty-four years from thence to the cutting off of Messiah, making four hundred and eighty-three years in all. Thus, there is one "week" left; and, according to the teaching which I find in this scripture, that must be the whole "week" in which antichrist sets up his rule, keeping the covenant for the first half, and becoming an oppressor in the second.

2. *Does 1 John iii. 1, 2, teach that the vision of Christ is to be the transforming power?*

Let us read the verses.

"Behold what manner of love the Father hath bestowed upon us, that we should be called children of God: and such we are. For this cause the world knoweth us not, because it knew Him not."

The question is concerned with what follows.

> "Beloved, now are we children of God, and it is not yet made manifest what we shall be. We know that, if He shall be manifested, we shall be like Him; for we shall see Him even as He is."

Now read verse 2 again, and substitute *because* as the exact equivalent of *for*. This will enable us to see that the statement may be taken in two ways. It may mean that we are quite sure we shall be like Christ, from the very fact that we are to see Him; or it may signify that seeing Him will cause us to be like Him. I do not dogmatize about these differing interpretations. While I long held and preached that the vision of Christ would change the believer, it now seems to me that this transformation must first take place; and the fact that I am to see Him is the proof that I shall be like Him. If my vision of Christ on the resurrection morning is to be the cause of my transformation, the pre-supposition is that I shall not be changed until I look at Him; that though the time be immeasurably short, yet my first view of Him will be in my unchanged condition. This is, in some aspects, a beautiful thought, but incorrect, as I think. I believe we shall be changed in a moment, in the twinkling of an eye; and that, when changed by the power of God, we shall look at Christ. John tells us that we shall be like Christ because only those bearing His likeness can see Him; and we are to have that blessed sight. It is the pure in heart who see God. I offer no hard and fast dictum on the point: but I find that almost all who have any right to deal with the original tongue lean to this exposition rather than to the other.

3. *What Scripture authority is there for supposing that some Christians may have to pass through the tribulation? Are not all believers members of the body of Christ?*

That is the question which has come from most places—India, Ireland, Scotland, Canada, and the United States, as well as from my own immediate neighborhood—showing that it has been exercising the minds of a large number of God's children. On the other hand, I may say before dealing with it that I have had many letters agreeing with the view I hold, that the Church is an elect body which is to be taken out of the world, while many Christians remain through the tribulation. It is difficult, briefly, to sketch the view which I derive from the New Testament. I must begin at a point which seems to be irrelevant, but I think you will see that it leads up to the answer. I only seek to lay before you the reasons for my conviction in this respect.

The truth concerning the Church or Body of

Jesus Christ is peculiar, as far as the teaching of the New Testament is concerned, to the writings of the apostle Paul. It is needful to remember that upon the statement just made is raised the structure which I commend to your notice. Jesus Christ did not preach about the Church at all. He went everywhere preaching the *Kingdom*, and He mentioned the Church only twice. Once, when He uttered a prophecy which was so magnificent as to embrace within itself all other prophecies concerning the Church, and yet was so simple that we can always remember it, He said to Peter, "Thou art a stone, and upon this Rock I will build my Church." We must never forget the distinct difference between a piece of stone, *petros*, and the solid rock, *petra*. The Church's security lies in its being built on the Rock, and its ultimate triumph as an aggressive force is declared in the words, "The gates of Hades shall not prevail against it"; "The last enemy that shall be abolished is death"—and therefore death is not to prevail against the Church. The other reference is when Christ speaks of discipline among His own disciples. If your offending brother refuses to hear you alone or in company with another, you are to bring the matter before the Church. In those two passages containing all that ever fell from Christ's lips on this point, we have (1) the Church's security;

Appendix

(2) its victorious conquest; and (3) its authority to excommunicate the man or woman who persists in sin.

New Testament writers others than Paul make no reference to the Catholic Church of the Firstborn, the great mystic Body of Christ; but only mention local churches, under the Greek word *Ecclesia*, meaning *assembly*. John writes about the Bride, but never names the Church. The Gospel of the Church was peculiarly and specially committed to Paul. May I ask you to follow me patiently through some of his statements on the subject. The Epistle to the Romans as to its argument ends with xvi. 23. Then follows the benediction, verse 24, in the Authorized, omitted from the Revised. The last three verses are undoubtedly Paul's words, but are an added doxology containing a very important statement, not worked out here, but in subsequent letters:

> "Now to Him that is able to stablish you according to MY GOSPEL and the preaching of Jesus Christ, according to the revelation of the *mystery* which hath been kept in silence through times eternal, but now is manifested, and by the scriptures of the prophets, according to the commandment of the eternal God, is made known unto all the nations unto obedience of faith; to the only wise God, through Jesus Christ, to Whom be the glory forever. Amen."

The apostle there made use of a remarkable phrase, "my gospel," in connection with an allusion to a mystery which he does not immediately unfold. That passage gives us the keyword "mystery." Now turn to 1 Cor. ii. 7–10.

> "But we speak God's wisdom in a *mystery*, even the wisdom that hath been hidden, which God foreordained before the worlds unto our glory : which none of the rulers of this world knoweth : for had they known it, they would not have crucified the Lord of glory : but as it is written, Things which eye saw not, and ear heard not, and which entered not into the heart of man, whatsoever things God prepared for them that love Him."

A common misquotation which I have heard made even by eminent preachers adds "to conceive" after "heart of man"; but it is unwarrantable to use the words as a statement by Paul that no one can have any idea of things to come. He has something more to say, and should not be interrupted; therefore read on :

> "But unto us God revealed them through the Spirit: for the Spirit searcheth all things, yea, the deep things of God."

Through the Holy Spirit this hidden mystery is to be understood, and it is to spiritual men only that it can ever be revealed.

A further step is taken in the epistles to the Ephesians and Colossians, where the mystery *is* unfolded.

> Eph. i. 9; iii. 1–4, 9: "Having made known unto us the *mystery* of His will, according to his good pleas-

ure which He purposed in Him. . . . For this cause I Paul, the prisoner of Christ Jesus in behalf of you Gentiles,—if so be that ye have heard of the dispensation of that grace of God which was given me to you-ward; how that by revelation was made known unto me the *mystery*, as I wrote afore in few words, whereby, when ye read, ye can perceive my understanding in the mystery of Christ; . . . and to make all men see what is the dispensation of the *mystery*," or, preferably, as the margin gives it, "the stewardship of the *mystery* which from all ages hath been hid in God."

Thus the apostle shows that the mystery hidden in past ages had been revealed to him; that he was commissioned to teach it; and that his was the stewardship of declaring it to the Church. In chapter v., where he has been speaking to husbands and wives, he says, concerning the great prototype of that relationship, " This *mystery* is great: but I speak in regard of Christ and of the Church " (verse 32). In vi. 19, 20, he asks for prayer, "that utterance may be given unto me in opening my mouth, to make known with boldness the *mystery* of the gospel, for which I am an ambassador in chains." Then, in his Epistle to the Colossians, Paul refers to the mystery and to its unfolding in another aspect.

Col. i. 26, 27: "Even the *mystery* which hath been hid from all ages and generations: but now hath it been manifested to His saints, to whom God was pleased to make known what is the riches of the glory of this

> *mystery* among the Gentiles, which is Christ in you, the hope of glory."
>
> ii. 2: "That their hearts may be comforted, they being knit together in love, and unto all riches of the full assurance of understanding, that they may know the *mystery* of God, even Christ."
>
> iv. 3: "Withal praying for us also, that God may open unto us a door for the word, to speak the *mystery* of Christ, for which I am also in bonds."

We have had the statement laid down that to Paul was committed the gospel of the mystery of the Church—of a people to be gathered out of the world and united, by the bonds of the very life of Christ, to Christ Himself, to be forevermore in such close association with Him, that the great apostle can only describe the union by speaking of Jesus as the Head, and of those gathered to Him as forming the Body. Such is the mystery that has come up from the eternities: that kings, rulers, and priests never saw; that apostles, even in the time of Jesus, did not understand; and that God committed to this one man.

After his conversion Paul was, first of all, united with those apostles who were called directly from Judaism; and for a certain period, in common with them, he preached the Gospel of the Kingdom. But there was a point where he ceased to proclaim the Kingdom, and began to preach "*my gospel*" of the Church. Careful reading of the Acts will show that in early days

Appendix

the first apostles were linked with Judaism; and it was through the revelation which God gave to Paul that there came a break between that system and the Church. It has been said that if Christ takes some Christians away and leaves others, it will rend His Body and break up the Church. Now, I have been very careful to avoid saying that members of the inner sacred Church of the Firstborn, or Christ's Body, will be left behind. Let me say emphatically that I believe the Body will not be rent, and that the Church of the Firstborn cannot be broken; that when the Master comes, the whole Church will go to meet Him. Who, then, will be left? Many Christian people who are not members of that Church of the Firstborn.

The question which naturally arises is, What constitutes membership of that Body? The answer is in a word—Election. Read the words of the man to whom was committed the Gospel of the Church:

> Rom. viii. 28-30: "We know that to them that love God all things work together for good, even to them that are called according to His purpose. For whom He foreknew, He also foreordained"—*predestined, as it is in the Authorized Version*—"and whom He foreordained, them He also called: and whom He called, them He also justified: and whom He justified, them He also glorified."

There you have the perfect working of God:

His sovereign, supreme election, from the past eternity right up to the glory, from eternity unto eternity: from the past sovereignty of God in foreknowing and foreordaining and selecting and electing—we cannot get away from these words, and must not be afraid of them—right on into the coming eternity, when God crowns His chosen with glory and honor. You read things like that in no writer save Paul: and he is referring to the Church, this company which God is gathering out into closest union with His Son. In the Book of Revelation you have the living creatures round the throne, with circle after circle of inhabitants beyond them. The living creatures mark the inner circle of the Church which God has selected, elected, chosen, and which Jesus is coming to gather unto Himself.

Now we ask, Whom does God foreordain? Read the words which I momentarily omitted from that passage in Romans: "*Foreordained to be conformed to the image of His Son.*" God's election of certain persons to constitute His Church is not capricious, but has regard to character. He foreordained those whom He foreknew, in order that they might be conformed to the image of His Son. Are there not hundreds of thousands of people in the world—forgive me, I will not say in the world, but in our churches—who are not conformed to

Appendix

the image of His Son? Assuredly there are. Are they not Christians? I think they are, I believe they are God's own children: but they are not conformed to the image of His Son, and will be left behind when the Master comes. He will gather out that inner mysterious unity, His own Catholic Church, made up of such men and women as He has predestined, foreordained; and He will gather them because they are conformed to the image of His Son. We must not make Paul's theology broader than it is in fact. Do not imagine that he writes about all Christian people; but remember that his subject is the inner circle of believers who are "blameless and harmless, without blemish in the midst of a crooked and perverse generation, among whom ye are seen as lights in the world." The whole of Paul's teaching is concerned with the Church; and the revelation of the mystery which he received when he was taken up into the third heaven has never been given to any other man save through his teaching. In that conception of the Church I find, for my own part, a solution of the apparent difficulty of the doctrine of election, and a very clear statement of the character of those who will be caught away to be with the Lord when He comes to gather His own.

Are there other scriptures favoring this view? I believe all the teaching of the Word to be in harmony therewith. Let us take two examples:

> Heb. ix. 27, 28: "And inasmuch as it is appointed unto men once to die, and after this cometh judgment; so Christ also, having been once offered to bear the sins of many, shall appear a second time, apart from sin, to them that wait for Him, unto salvation."

Christ will appear the second time, apart from sin, to them that WAIT for Him. The force of the teaching here is intensified by the Revised Version, in which "*wait*" is substituted for "*look*." Are there not hundreds of Christians who are not waiting for Him, and who would say: "Do not talk to us about these things; we do not believe in them, and do not wish to wait for Him"? There are scores of Christian people to whom the certainty of Christ's coming to-morrow morning would bring consternation. If there is one thing they would wish to postpone, it is that coming. As I have already shown, those who are truly waiting for Christ are not star-gazers, but men and women conformed to His likeness, living as He did, doing His work, watching for Him in the midst of active service.

Certain expositors tell us that of the virgins (Matt. xxv.) five were good and five bad. Nay, verily. The five foolish virgins were separated from the crowd and had lamps and oil. Their lamps were not *gone*, but *going*, out.

They had everything necessary, but not a sufficiency. When the five wise virgins had gone into the wedding and the five foolish ones knocked at the door, the Master said, "I know you not": that is to say, He had shut the door upon them as far as that dispensation was concerned; but they were not lost. Jesus said, "*The Kingdom of heaven* is likened unto *ten virgins*," not the Kingdom of heaven, unto five; and the kingdom of earth, unto five. In the following parable of the talents, a number of men are needed for another picture of the Kingdom of heaven. It was one of the Lord's own servants who did not use the one talent, but buried it, and was consequently turned into outer darkness. There is no reason to suppose that the "outer darkness" refers to Gehenna, the place of eternal loss; but to the tribulation, in contrast to the light in the marriage chamber of the Lamb.

We cannot dwell upon the interesting study, but it may well teach us the importance of careful reading. Let us not imagine that we know all contained in this Book of God. For myself, I find that a single verse will often hold me in a way that permits no escape from it. Every time a man gets on his knees before God, with this Book in his hand, he will make fresh discoveries of his own ignorance. We cannot read it as we would peruse the latest novel:

for the Book of God will demand careful search, patient attention, and continued labor with heart and mind if we are to know it. I have dealt at much length with this question of believers passing through the tribulation, because of its great importance in my own view, and having regard to the wide interest indicated by the many quarters from which it has come.

4. *What relation do little children bear to the truth of the Lord's coming?*

A beautiful question, to which, however, no definite answer can be given from Scripture, save by deduction and inference. I gather from the work and words of Jesus that all children who have not willfully sinned will be taken away from the tribulation, and that irrespective of parentage. I believe that the children of the most ungodly men and women in the world are Christ's by virtue of what He accomplished upon the Cross. There is a point at which such children will need to be born again from above, and that is, when they reach the place of responsibility. I have a boy in my own home who certainly has not yet reached that point; and my personal conviction of the tenderness of the heart of my God assures me (but I speak without dogmatism even here) that if He should take me, He would not leave my child, who has no knowledge of right and wrong, to pass through the tribulation. I simply rely upon my own view of the great heart of God and the work and words of Jesus Christ.

5. *In view of prophecy, how near may the coming of Christ be?*

I have said again and again that no man can fix the date of the advent of Christ. According to Mr. Dimbleby, the times of the Gentiles end upon Good Friday in this present Eastertide (1898). He was very careful to guard himself against any assumption that the Parousia would take place then. I neither affirm nor deny his conclusion; but I do say that we have no single line of teaching which conclusively proves the place or time of Christ's coming. In Daniel's image we have the head of gold, representing the Babylonian empire; the breast and arms of silver, as the Medo-Persian kingdom; the belly and thighs of brass, as the Macedonian monarchy; and the legs of iron, as the Roman rule. There can be no doubt that all these have been fulfilled and have passed away. The feet and toes, a mixture of iron and of clay, are in the times of the fullness of the Gentiles; and all the rest of the image is gone. How is this image to end? By the Stone cut without hands out of the mountain, striking the feet and breaking the whole thing into pieces. The image is simply symbolical of earthly power, to be ended by the coming of Jesus Christ, not *for* but *with* His people. He will come and take His Church away, and then seven years must pass before the Stone will smite the image unto its destruction. That issue, however, does not fix the time of our Lord's coming for his people, which may be before the ten toes (kingdoms) have run their course, or afterward. All we know is, that before the image of worldly power can be demolished, Christ, the Stone cut without hands from the mountain, must smite that image. But no man knoweth the day or the hour of Christ's coming; consequently, the only word which He speaks to His own people is, "Watch: for in such an hour as ye know not the Son of Man cometh!"

6. *Can we hasten the coming of the Lord? If so, how?*

In 2 Peter iii. 11, 12, we have words bearing on that question.

"Seeing that these things are thus all to be dissolved, what manner of persons ought ye to be in all holy living and godliness, looking for and earnestly desiring the coming of the day of God."

In the Authorized Version you have it "hastening unto," but the marginal reading of the

Revised Version is, I believe, far nearer the original idea than either of the others—" earnestly *hastening* the coming of the day of God." Yes, I think it is possible to hasten the coming of the Master, by His Bride being ready for Him, as it has been put in that hymn of El Nathan's:

> Let all that look for, hasten
> The coming joyful day,
> By earnest consecration,
> To walk the narrow way.

The moment His Bride—the Body, the Church—is ready, He will come. I believe that is the true force of the word in the Epistle of Peter—not hastening unto, but "hastening" the coming.

7. *When the present dispensation ends, and the Spirit is withdrawn, will His office and work, as set forth in John xiv., xv., xvi., be superseded by the personal ministry of Christ? When the Spirit is gone, who will carry on His work?*

The Spirit is withdrawn only in a dispensational sense. Every successive age with which we have dealt on the Chart included within itself all that had gone before; and the Millennium will have in it all the richness, glory, and beauty, of everything that has preceded it. The Spirit will be withdrawn in this one way—as a presence in the world which prevents the full outworking of evil. Immediately the Spirit is withdrawn, antichrist will work mightily through the seven years; but in the Millennium, itself, it is by the same Holy Spirit that men will be brought into living contact with Jesus Christ.

8. *To what does Enoch's prophecy refer, as recorded in Jude?*

To the coming of the Lord to set up His kingdom upon the earth. "Behold the Lord came with ten thousand of His holy ones, to execute judgment upon all."

9. *What judgment is referred to in Matt. xxv. in the parable of the sheep and the goats? And at what period in your Chart does that judgment come?*

There is nothing more commonly misinterpreted than that parable. It contains no single word about the dead; but is exactly what it professes to be—a picture of the time when Christ shall come and all *nations* shall be gathered before Him. It is the judgment, not of individuals, nor of the Church, but of the nations of the earth, when Christ comes at the end of Jacob's trouble. The basis of judgment for the nations is to be their treatment of Christ's brethren, the Israelitish nation. Of course, in all Jewish truth there is an undercurrent of application to God's children in general; but we should be careful how we apply the words "Inasmuch as ye did it unto one of these my brethren, even these least, ye did it unto Me." They do not belong to this dispensation, but to the next; and there is nothing in them which has any very close bearing upon our present position.

10. *Who will be the victims of the final apostasy after the thousand years?*

It is distinctly stated in Rev. xx. 7, 8, that when Satan is loosed, he will deceive *the nations.* During that period of the Millennial reign, the nations will be subject to Christ, but not all of them will be loyal in heart to Him ; and when Satan is loosed, it will be to deceive such disloyal nations. That the obedience to the government of Christ during the Millennial period will be feigned is clearly taught in such passages as Psalms xviii. 44 and lxvi. 3, where the Hebrew word translated "submit" is the same translated elsewhere, "deceive," "dissemble," "deal falsely," "lie." All the nations will be under the government of the "Rod of iron," and will be compelled to submit therefore. In heart, however, the great mass will be rebellious to the end, and will eagerly avail themselves of the opportunity of outwardly throwing off the yoke and entering upon actual conflict, when it presents itself in the unloosing of Satan.

11. *Is there any possibility of a raptured saint being deceived and finally lost?*

Absolutely no possibility, because the raptured saints will have entered into a state which shall fit them for the New Jerusalem, into which nothing that worketh abomination or maketh a lie can come—that is, there will be for them no further temptation to sin. This, of itself, answers the other part of the question— Would Heb. vi. 4-7 refer to such a time? Certainly not.

12. *1 Cor. xv. 24-27; Rev. xx. 14. Do not these Scriptures, taken in conjunction, teach that Christ delivers up the Kingdom at the destruction of death, before the new heavens and the new earth?*

I do not think that is a necessary sequence. The "then" of Corinthians does not mean immediate action. There is another "then" which bears out my view, in verse 23. "Each in his own order: Christ the first-fruits; *then* they that are Christ's at His coming. Then cometh the end." That is, as I believe, in the period of which we have no measurement, beyond the great white throne, and beyond the creation of the new heavens and the new earth.

Appendix

13. *Does the final triumph of Jesus Christ include the ultimate reconciliation and subjection of every soul of man to Him so that not one shall be utterly and eternally lost?*

My correspondent uses two words, "reconciliation" and "subjection." The final triumph of Jesus *does* include the "subjection" of every soul of man to Him; for, God has exalted Christ "that at the name of Jesus *every* knee should bow, and that *every* tongue should confess that Jesus Christ is Lord, to the glory of God the Father." But the final triumph of Jesus Christ does not necessarily include the "reconciliation" of every soul to Him. There will be souls unreconciled who will yet be subject. It is an awful topic to deal with; but the possibility is clearly taught in the New Testament that a soul may, by its own free will, be alienated from Jesus Christ; and that, nevertheless, He may have out of that soul the honor which comes from subjection apart from reconciliation. In passing, and in connection with the great theme which we are only touching upon, let me say to Bible students that we must be very careful how we use the word "eternity." We have fallen into great error in our constant use of that word. There is no word in the whole Book of God corresponding with our "eternal," which, as commonly used among us, means absolutely without end. The strongest

Scripture word used with reference to the existence of God, is—"unto the ages of the ages," which does not literally mean eternally. Let us, however, remember that the self-same word, which is thus used in connection with the existence of God, is also applied to the loss of the human soul. Men have divided the Church, separated from each other, and persecuted one another, upon a thought conveyed by an English word which has no equivalent in the Bible. But who shall grasp "the ages of the ages," or say that when a limit is reached, if limit there be, it is not that other ages upon ages may be born? God is subject to no limitation, and our finite thought must utterly fail to fathom the ages which He inhabits. We have no right to dogmatize upon anything beyond what is written; nor should we use a human word to express Divine things in the great future, concerning which we know so little. I repeat, it is a solemn possibility that a soul may, by its own deliberate, unchanging choice, pass into the ages of the ages, without God and without hope, and yet be subject to Christ, while unreconciled to Him.

14. *According to 1 Cor. xv. 26, the last enemy that shall be destroyed is death. What about him that hath the power of death?*

We are told that Satan has the power of

Appendix

death—and I take the inference of my correspondent to be this: if death is the last thing to be abolished, then the one who has the power of it must first be abolished. I venture to think that what is implied in the question does not follow. In the passage referred to, we have enemies *under Christ's feet*, and enemies *abolished*. There may be enemies who will never be abolished, though they be under His feet. Christ must reign until He has put *all* enemies under His feet. Lucifer, the son of the morning, must be put under His feet. And so must the souls of men who deliberately rebel against Him; but it is not said that He shall abolish them. He will abolish death; and, in that case, there can be no dying, even for rebel souls.

I have endeavored to answer the whole of the questions selected according to the light which I have. We now, for the present, take leave of this great subject of prophecy. Maintaining the spirit of readiness for Divine leading in regard to lines of teaching, we may, at a future day, return to the subject in some other aspect. But, in conclusion, let me say that truth should never make us proud. We may be very confident that we hold the truth; but the surest way to deny its power is to be bitter and unloving toward those who differ from us.

Let us remember that Truth is Christ, and Christ is Truth; that Christ is God, and God is Love; therefore Truth is Love, and Love is Truth. In proportion as you may hold the Truth, you will become loving toward those who differ from you. All the wrangling, ostensibly for the sake of Truth, which has split and divided certain sections of the Church, until men therein scarcely know where they stand, is evidence that Truth has never been properly understood by them. Truth should not be stored as a commodity or as something of which to boast. While we feel that the teaching of the Word of God is very clear, let us remember that we are only scholars spelling out the alphabet in the school of Jesus Christ. We may rest assured that, in the day when we have full knowledge granted unto us, we shall discover that the men of whom we were the most afraid, have held Truth which we, perchance, have never known. Our duty toward our brother and his toward us, if we be loyal to Christ, is—that we love each other still, though we may not agree in our views. Should nothing else be accomplished by this series of lectures, we may be profoundly thankful if they lead to searching of the Word of God.

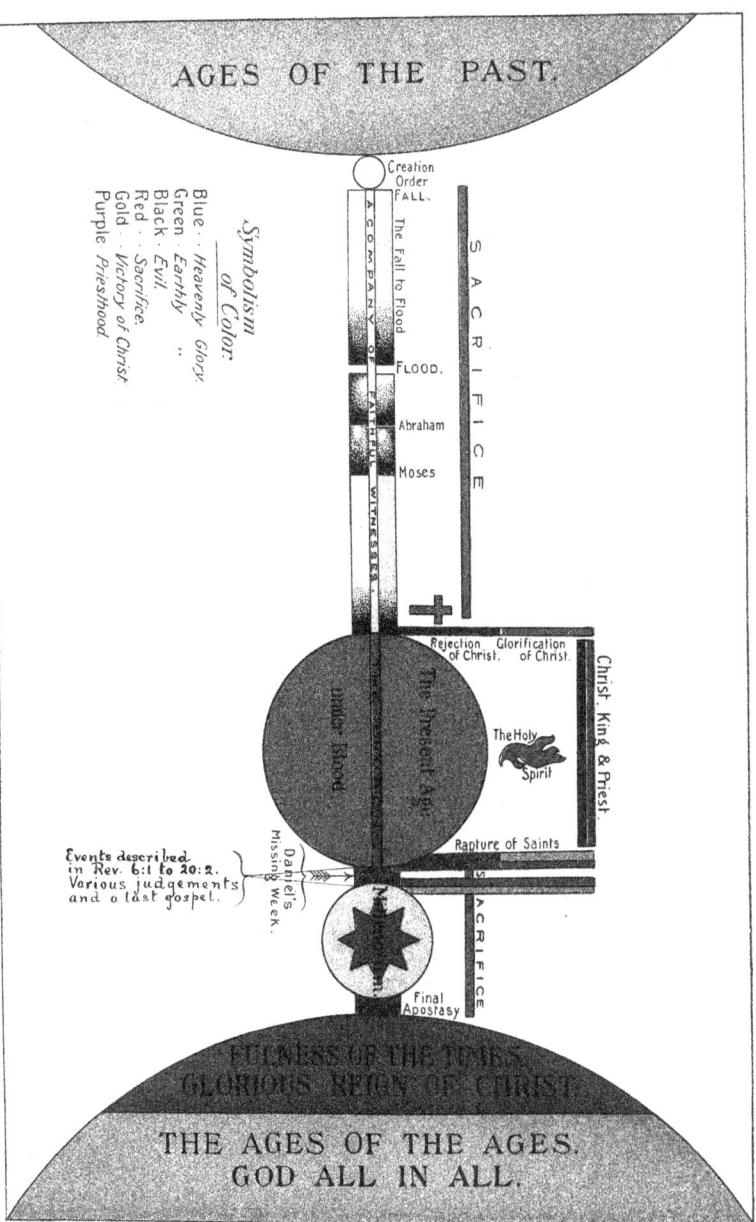

CHART OF EVENTS, PAST, PRESENT, AND FUTURE.

www.ingramcontent.com/pod-product-compliance
Lightning Source LLC
Chambersburg PA
CBHW051057160426
43193CB00010B/1226